Congratulations on your

graduation from high school.

Success always —

the Youngs

1974

Now
and
Forever

Now and Forever

MARION D. HANKS

ILLUSTRATIONS BY BILL KUHRE

Published by
BOOKCRAFT, INC.
Salt Lake City, Utah

Library of Congress Catalog Card Number: 74-75165

ISBN 0-88494-212-0

1st Printing, 1974

LITHOGRAPHED IN U.S.A.
PUBLISHERS PRESS
SALT LAKE CITY, UTAH

Dedication

By special invitation my wife and I were in attendance in the meeting in our ward when our only son was presented to the congregation to receive the Aaronic Priesthood and be ordained to the office of deacon. At home that afternoon he was explaining the experience to his four sisters. They asked him if he felt uneasy standing with the bishop in front the congregation when the vote was taken.

"A little," he said, "but I looked down and saw Dad's hand higher than all the rest, and I felt all right."

It was true; my hand was held as high as I could reach. He is my son, and that's how I feel about him. I feel that way about his sisters, too, and the great generation the five of them represent.

So to our five, and the choice, glowing group of which they are part, this book is dedicated as a vote of respect, affection, and confidence.

And the hand is as high as I can reach.

Preface

By career, by calling, and by personal choice my life has brought me the privilege of extensive association with youth in and out of the Church. In classrooms, on athletic courts, in gatherings large and small, and in private interview, it has been my blessing to come in touch with their strengths and weaknesses, their hopes and fears, their joy and their heartbreak. I have learned of their aspirations and ambitions and have seen their accomplishments and their failures. It has been manifest to me, with force and great satisfaction, that when the mantle of leadership falls to them from older shoulders, the solid majority of them will be capable and worthy of bearing it.

Youth of such promise needs to be especially alert to the path and its pitfalls. With this interest at heart I have from time to time written brief pieces which I believe my young friends can readily relate to. Some of these pieces have now been gathered into this book.

There is no thought that here are all the answers to youth's needs. Far from it. It is my hope however that the young reader will accept it as a sincere effort by one who, through experience and the witness of the Spirit, knows the importance of the true way and is anxious to help others along that road. How you travel that road is of vital significance to you — now and forever.

Contents

1

Get Ready

Some people seem to think that pioneering and exploring and adventuring are finished, that the world is "on the brink," just holding still for the explosion that will push it over. Some seemingly suppose (and unfortunately their attitude is contagious) that there isn't any use in planning or preparing.

Youth knows better.

Young people know that many great books haven't yet been written, the best songs haven't been sung, the best planes are not yet engineered, the roads for the future haven't been built. They see the Church growing amazingly. They have seen a missionary teaching effort in the last few years that is bringing wonderful results. They know that this is a good time to be alive—a great day!

All the good things of all past ages are here to be enjoyed and built upon. Great advances lie ahead. In medicine, science, space, energy, environment, human relationships, and in man's spiritual search, the frontiers are expanding.

The young are preparing! They know that the adventures ahead will require trained minds, strong bodies, sound nerves, disciplined emotions, courageous hearts, and spirits prayerfully and humbly in tune with Almighty God. They will be ready!

But youth is *you!* How are things with you?

We know that *you* know that worthwhile lives, like good buildings, must have sound foundations, that the job of building your foundation is mostly up to *you,* and that the time to be putting the materials together is *now*.

One of the things that will help you most is an appreciation of how *important you are*—not in any arrogant, proud, "big me" sense, of course, but humbly because you are a choice child of God, a fine human being with a pattern all of your own which has never been exactly duplicated and never will be. You are not just like any of your friends or family or anyone else. You have abilities and resources that are very valuable and greatly needed and the opportunity and responsibility to develop them. You matter very much for what you are, and for what you are going to be.

You matter—now and forever!

2

Eyes Like Helen,

Has your school paper recently published (or have you heard other young people talking about) a conglomerate All-American Boy or All-American Girl? You know, a smile like John, hair like Tom, muscles like Richard—or teeth like Jane, personality like Mary, eyes like Helen. There may have been reference to school activity, loyalty, enthusiasm, good sportsmanship, religious leadership, integrity, initiative, ability to plan and use time wisely, but many of these are often left out, unfortunately.

No Such "Animal"

Has it occurred to you that there is no such creature as this imaginary All-American Boy or Girl?

3

The fact is that there isn't, which is the reason why one has to be pasted together, of course. There is no living model we could follow to fashion a perfect boy or girl. These are those with admirable qualities or attributes or features, and there can be value and virtue in admiring them and learning from them. What all of us must soon or late learn, though, is that each human being is endowed with certain basic materials and the chance to use them and develop them, and there can't be any trading or buying or borrowing of those materials.

Smile Like John...

Harm or Help?

Is there harm in piecing together an "ideal" boy or girl as a dream or ambition, or as a journalistic effort for the school paper, or a subject for conversation? Probably not. Such a manufactured "ideal" can be good if it helps us establish high and wholesome and realistic objectives. But it can be bad if some wonderful young person, choice child of God, gets discouraged or disheartened because he or she isn't just like the "ideal," and maybe begins to feel inadequate or left out or hopeless or worthless. Then the project can be destructive and unwise.

There is nothing we can do personally about the particular building blocks with which each of us starts life. There is everything we can do about recognizing and accepting and improving and using well what we have been given!

Be Yourself

So you don't have Mary's friendly personality or John's smile —they probably wouldn't be natural or good on you, anyway! You have a fine, pleasing smile of your own, if you'll use it more freely and with more confidence. And personality?—why that is simply an expression of what is distinctive and individual about you. Your personality can be developed to represent what you genuinely are, what you sincerely want to be, what you earnestly are trying to become. It can't be just like the personality of anyone else; you wouldn't really want it to be; the result would be artificial and unnatural.

Your Very Best Self

You must begin by accepting the fact that you are what you are, and then setting to work to be the very best you can be. You are a thinking, communicating, choice, eternal child of God. You are free to choose, to dream, to plan, free to work, to learn, to grow. Because you are *who* you are and *what* you are, your ceiling is unlimited. Your objective is to know yourself, value yourself, improve yourself, share yourself, be yourself. Start now to reach and to achieve. There won't be a better time.

His Own Mind

The young Mormon marine was uneasy
and didn't know why. There were
plenty of ordinary reasons for a member of a combat unit in almost daily
contact with the enemy to feel uneasy,
but this was something different.
When he returned with his group to
their base camp after several days in
the field, he discovered what it was.

"C'mon, Smith," the sergeant said. "The whole
outfit's going into town. This time you're coming
with us even if we have to drag you. You are
about to find out how big men live when they get
away from their mamas."

Rick Smith caught the sharp edge of the other's
voice, knifing through the seeming lightness of his
words. He understood the look in the eye and the tightness at
the corners of the mouth. Sarge wasn't kidding; he really intended
to take Rick along, even if he had to drag him.

"No thanks, Sarge," Rick said. "I'm staying here."

"Listen, Sonny," came the grim answer, "big men can make
up their own minds about their lives. They don't stay tied to
Mommy's apron strings when they're in this man's outfit. You're
coming with us."

Rick Smith could feel the color drain from his face and the
strength ebb from his knees, but his voice surprised him with its
calmness as he heard himself answer:

"You're right, Sarge, a big man can make up his own mind. I have the responsibility to decide whether I'll live the way you do or the way I believe in. You've made *your* choice, Sergeant, and that's your business. But I still have a choice, and I prefer to live another way. That's what I've made up my mind to do. I'm staying here."

The sergeant turned on his heel, muttering curses. Elder Richard Smith, nineteen, found a quiet place, and in his loneliness he thanked God in his heart for an answer he had been afraid he might not know how to give. He'd been uneasy because he had somehow known intuitively that there was a different kind of battle ahead of him that day. He was sure now that there were more battles to come, but he'd won this one, and he was grateful.

6

"Make It a Good Day!"

Five Things To Accomplish

7

First, *learn how to use your head. Learn to work at learning and love it. Information may become irrelevant; the capacity to learn gains in importance.*

Second, *develop the power to appreciate life on a broad basis, with social and cultural skills learned and practiced under favorable conditions, with good companions.*

Third, *acquire that sense of wholeness that accompanies honest self-respect—the self-esteem that comes with wise choices acted upon, or, when they are poor, repented of.*

Fourth, *have a genuine concern for others—an identification with others. Learn how to love and express love wisely and well, and learn to "bridle all your passions that ye may be filled with love."* (Alma 38:12.)

Fifth, *learn to trust God and to serve him, to rest in him, to walk humbly before him, and to be confident in his presence.*

A good friend who is the president of a university supplied an idea that I would like to share. He was visiting with a former student in another country, and as he left his young associate one day, heard him say, "Make it a good day!"

He turned back and asked, "What did you say?"

The young man replied, "I said, 'Make it a good day!' "

In many of our homes and among many of us there is the usual and appropriate expression as we depart from each other, "Have a good day!" What he said was a little different: "Make it a good day!"

For all of you, may I offer that earnest invitation: Make it a good day! Make it a good experience. Make it a happy, wholesome, memorable, lifelong good experience. There are ways to do that—you can, you know, if you will. There is no guarantee that all will, but you can.

Samuel Johnson put a finger on the possibility and path in two very significant statements. First, the last four lines added by Johnson to a poem by Oliver Goldsmith:

> *How small, in all that human hearts endure,*
> *That part which laws or kings can cause or cure.*
> *Still to ourselves, in every place consigned,*
> *Our own felicity we make or find.*

The other thought:

> *The fountain of content must spring up in the mind, and he who has so little knowledge of human nature as to seek happiness by changing anything but his own disposition will waste his life in fruitless effort and multiply the griefs which he purposes to remove.*

There is, Johnson believed (and I believe), in the grasp of each of us the power and probability of making it a good day, a good family, a good society, and a good world. How do you go about that?

Somebody wrote that "no life can be truly great [and I think he did not mean famous or spectacular] until it is focused, dedicated and disciplined."

David Starr Jordan gave us this short and significant paragraph:

8

To choose among the different possible courses of action is the primary function of the intellect. To choose at all implies the choice of the best. In the long run only those who choose the best survive. The best each one must find out for himself. To choose the best is the art of existence—of all the fine arts, this is the finest and noblest. By the best, we mean that which makes for abundance of life for ourselves and for others.

Now, whether or not it is a good day—whether you make it a good day, a good experience, a good life—will depend upon what you choose to believe in, to serve, and to be.

Do you remember what Paul wrote to the Philippians (to paraphrase): "Brethren, I do not claim to have attained or apprehended. I am not perfect, and I certainly do not understand everything." But he understood something. What was it?

. . . but this one thing I do, forgetting those things which are behind, and reaching forth unto those things which are before, I press toward the mark for the prize of the high calling of God in Christ Jesus."

—Philippians 3:13-14.

He did not know everything, and he had not achieved everything, but he had wisdom enough to leave the past behind when it was not contributing to his strength, and to move forward with what he now had.

9

Somebody wrote recently: "History is what men make it." You can make it a good day—a good experience, a good family, a good life—if you want to enough, and try hard enough.

There is a fact so obvious that it would seem hard to avoid if one were thinking—yet many individuals, young and older, seem not to be conscious of it.

It is that we choose the *conclusion* of an act when we choose to perform the act; we agree to the *results* of a decision when we make it; we select a *destination* when we start on a path or trail.

"He who picks up one end of a stick picks up the other. He who chooses the beginning of a road chooses the place it leads to."
—Harry Emerson Fosdick

The wise Solomon said:

"Ponder the path of thy feet, and let all thy ways be established."
—Proverbs 4:26. See Verses 23-27

Which roads are you walking? Have you

10

Where the Path Leads

considered carefully the places they lead to?

Have you pondered "the path of thy feet?"

Are you thinking with your mind—and not with your desires or envy or emotion?

Who, understanding that at the end of the path of clean conduct and cheerful obedience lies self-respect and quiet conscience and "joy unspeakable," would not choose to walk that way instead of some other? . . .

if she were thinking straight!

What one of us, aware of the destination for those who are honest and dependable and have integrity, would not rush to the road leading to it? . . .

if we were thinking maturely!

Which boy or girl, anxious for real happiness in a good home with a worthy companion and fine family, would neglect the day-by-day things that lead to them? . . .

if he or she were thinking well!

Who would not choose to prepare for a mission, realizing what lies at the end of that great spiritual adventure in faith and service? . . .

if he were thinking right!

What individual, knowing the joy of activity and full fellow-ship in the kingdom of God with the Saints, would follow mis-direction to the bypaths of foolish habits or corroding resentments or unworthy companionships? . . .

if he were thinking wisely!

Which one, having sinned and knowing his need for the mercy and love and long-suffering of God, would not choose the road of repentance and forgiveness rather than continuing in the path of unrighteousness? . . .

11

if he were thinking clearly!

Look to the road you are walking on! Consider what lies at the end of it.

"Ponder the path of thy feet"—and, where necessary, turn back.

Pray for help to think clearly and walk wisely.

"Teach me thy way, O Lord, and lead me in a plain path, . . . "

—Psalm 27:11

Think with your mind, seek the Spirit of the Lord, look to the end of the road.

And as you look and ponder and pray, listen for the voice—

"And thine ears shall hear a word behind thee, saying, This is the way, walk ye in it, when ye turn to the right hand, and when ye turn to the left."

—Isaiah 30:21

A Football Star *who knew which things mattered most and chose to serve them*

12

A few years ago a rugged Mormon boy, Gilbert Tobler, gained wide honors playing football for the University of Utah. He was an all-around athlete whose qualities made him an attractive possibility for professional sports. One day, at the conclusion of his college career, Gil brought a visitor to Temple Square and accompanied him with a guide on a tour of the grounds. The visitor was a representative of a professional football organization who had come hoping to sign Gil to play for his team.

I asked Gil if he had received an offer, and if he intended to accept it. He answered that he had received an offer but had not accepted it. I asked him if the inducements were not enough, and he replied that they were very attractive and included the possibility of help in getting a medical education during his off-season months. Why would he reject such an offer? *"Because,"* he said, *"I have been called on a mission and I have accepted that call."*

The next time I saw Gil Tobler he had completed an honorable and very successful mission in South Africa, had finished his medical schooling, and was pursuing his training as a specialist. At the same time he was serving as president of a small branch of Chinese and Polynesian Saints—in his modest, manly way serving the Lord and his fellowmen. He had early in his life settled on his purpose and principles and would not turn away from them through the lure of attractive temporal goals or material possessions.

Now living in Salt Lake City working as an orthopedic specialist, Dr. Gilbert Tobler and his family are active, faithful members of the Church, still choosing to serve the " . . . things that matter most."

13

Dr. Tobler has been a Bishop and is presently serving as chairman of the Athletic Committee of the Melchizedek Priesthood MIA for the Church.

Then Shall the King Say

unto them on his right hand, Come, ye blessed of my Father, inherit the Kingdom prepared for you from the foundation of the world:

14

FOR I WAS AN HUNGRED, *and ye gave me meat:* I WAS THIRSTY, *and ye gave me drink:* I WAS A STRANGER, *and ye took me in:* NAKED, *and ye clothed me:* I WAS SICK *and ye visited me:* I WAS IN PRISON, *and ye came unto me.*

Then shall the righteous answer him, saying, Lord, when saw we thee an hungred, and fed thee? or thirsty, and gave thee drink?
When saw we thee a stranger, and took thee in? or naked, and clothed thee?
Or when saw we thee sick, or in prison and came unto thee?

And the King shall answer and say unto them, Verily, I say unto you, Inasmuch as ye have done it unto one of the least of these my brethren, ye have done it unto me.
Matthew
25:34-40

I was thirsty...

Rosalie was new in the ward. At fifteen this can be a problem. Everyone had his own friends. All the groups were settled. Everyone knew for sure just which boys or girls went around together. They all went to the same school. And they'd all lived in the same area for ages, it seemed. They had so much in common. They had so many things to talk about, so much to laugh at. They looked so busy with plans to make and places to go and the weekend's activities to report on. It was like being surrounded by water but not being able to drink.

Being new to Rosalie meant being out of it. She wished her parents had never moved away from the ward where she had become converted to the Church and where she had felt so welcomed. How thirsty she was for friends and fun and a feeling of belonging!

It was just before Christmas, and the holiday held no excitement for her. She had promised herself last night as she finished her prayers that if things weren't better at church this week, she'd never come back again. She just couldn't take any more sitting alone, having no one to talk with, no one to walk to class with. Oh, the kids had said hello that first time, and the teacher had welcomed her, but that was the end of that.

What Rosalie didn't know was that someone else had also been praying last night. Her mother sensed this trying problem in Rosalie's life and had earnestly asked Heavenly Father to help, to touch someone's heart that they might take this young girl in so she wouldn't be lost to the kingdom.

That Sunday when Rosalie slipped into her place on one side of the chapel, she wasn't alone for long. One of the most popular girls in the ward left the familiar group she always came in with and walked over toward Rosalie.

"Hi!" She smiled broadly as she sat down beside her. "May I sit here?"

"Oh, yes, do! Isn't Christmas a happy time?" Rosalie uttered a silent prayer of thanks that there was one girl in the many who would bother to offer just the kind of drink that would quench her particular thirst.

15

I was strange...

It isn't unusual to see a woman's eyes glow with that special luminosity of mother love when a child's warm squeeze around the neck emphasizes the pronouncement, "I love you!"

But when Karen Miles witnessed that sweet scene between Susannah and little Jeannie, it was different. Susannah was a troubled visitor in the Miles home, far away from her own children, and Jeannie was Karen's tiny daughter. Susannah had been ill and was deeply depressed, and the Miles family had been concerned for her and praying earnestly for her recovery since Dad had brought her home two days before Christmas. Her response to Jeannie's spontaneous outpouring of affection was the first expression of a willingness to give or receive love that the Miles family had seen.

Robert Miles was troubled when he first called Karen to tell her about Susannah. He knew of his family's involvements during the holiday season, and he was reluctant to impose upon them. But Susannah had come to him ill and away from her family, and he couldn't turn her away. He had tried to find a solution in time to get her home for Christmas, but circumstances made that impossible. He just couldn't put her into a hotel or hospital for Christmas, so he had called Karen, and his wife had responded graciously and generously, as she always did.

Thus Susannah spent the Christmas holidays at the Miles home. At first she was unhappy and ill at ease. The dark moods came on her and she wept and was afraid. She seemed alien and suspicious; she would not be one of them no matter how they tried. The older children responded to their parents' invitation to make special efforts to be kind, but they were rebuffed. Bob and Karen earnestly entreated the Lord, and made plans for medical help after Christmas, but they began to despair as the situation seemed to stay the same. Then came Christmas morning and Jeannie, and the miracle occurred.

Susannah had accepted her presents gratefully, but that curtain over her eyes shut them out, and the faraway look made them aware that the gifts, however graciously given, were poor sub-

---

This story about Susannah (names changed) is true and actually happened to the Hanks family.

stitutes for the love and acceptance of her own family. Then, without invitation or warning, Jeannie climbed on Susannah's lap, put her plump little arms around her neck, kissed her, and said, "Susannah, I lub you." Other little ones followed her lead, climbing and laughing and loving the guest whose troubles they didn't understand but whose presence they appreciated. The parents watched in wonder as the curtain in Susannah's eyes dissolved in believing tears, and a child's guileless love turned the key to a heart long afraid.

So Karen Miles wept, and her husband and older children did, too.

Days later, when Susannah had gone to rejoin her own family, Robert read at family night a verse of scripture that now had great meaning to the Miles family. They had begun to understand why it had been such a great Christmas—the one that in future years they would often refer to as their best. They had thought they were going out of their way and giving, but in truth they had been the ones most blessed. They had celebrated Christmas in the best possible way, forgetful of self, worshiping Christ, giving, sharing, sacrificing their own plans, praying, trying to help another. That's why the scripture made such sense:

"Be not forgetful to entertain strangers: for thereby some have entertained angels unawares." (Hebrews 13:2.)

"... I was a stranger, and ye took me in." (Matthew 25:35.)

I was naked...

The young man walked resolutely down the city street to the clothing store, his hand in his pocket holding tightly to the five twenty-dollar bills wadded together there. He couldn't afford to lose them—they represented the new suit and overcoat he would wear on his mission. Like most of the rest of the money for his mission, the hundred dollars had been slowly, painfully accumulated through his own efforts. With careful planning and determined budgeting the money would see him through his two years of special service to the Lord.

He was startled when the man stopped in front of him, and would have walked around him, but the smile and outstretched

17

The names in this true story about a missionary were changed for previous publication. Actually, "Stanley Hale" was Stanley A. Hanks, "Anthon Van Orden" was Anthon Alrich, and "Marsden Hale" was Marion D. Hanks.

hand brought the face and slight frame into focus. It was Anthon Van Orden, a friend of his father before he died many years ago.

Brother Van Orden had been kind to the Hale family through the years. A Thanksgiving turkey, a Christmas box, an occasional envelope with a few dollars for Mother.

Now he inquired of the younger man's health and current activities. Marsden found himself answering reluctantly, almost evasively. He didn't want Brother Van Orden to feel that he was expected to offer financial help. Reluctantly he revealed the facts under the older man's questioning.

Yes, it was about time he was going on a mission. Yes, he had been called. Yes, he was going soon. As a matter of fact, he was in the mission home right now, preparing to leave. Yes, he was on the way to purchase some needed items for his mission. Yes, he did happen to be looking for a suit and an overcoat. Yes, he guessed he could take a few minutes to accompany Brother Van Orden into the more expensive store across the street.

The family friend seemed pleased at the chance meeting, but Marsden was uneasy. He knew that the older man rented rooms in his modest home and that he had modest employment; Marsden didn't want to exact or accept sacrifice from him. He protested the journey en route, but Brother Van Orden smilingly insisted.

In the store an expensive suit, coat, and hat were selected. Marsden demurred—they cost too much, it wasn't necessary. But Brother Van Orden insisted; Stanley Hale's son was to have the best. He seemed so excited and pleased and anxious to do this, and Marsden, having protested enough, gratefully thanked him.

"Before you go," said the older man, "let me tell you why this privilege means so much to me.

"I came to this country as an immigrant boy of fourteen. I didn't speak the language; I had no money and no job and no friends. I was frightened, but determined to make good in this new glorious land. Someone sent me to Stanley Hale. 'He takes in strays,' they said. I did not then understand the meaning of that, but I understood the heart of your father. He found me a job. He brought blankets so I could sleep on the couch in his office. He brought food for me until I could buy my own.

"I have been waiting a long time to tell that story to Stanley Hale's youngest child. I have been waiting a long time to return to Stanley Hale's son a little of the bread his sainted father cast upon the waters for me many years ago. Today you have made me very happy, and I weep with joy."

Marsden Hale's eyes were moist, too, as he pondered the miracle of bread upon the waters, of a neighbor fed and clothed in time of need.

In his heart he thanked God for a father he had never known, but now seemed to know so well.

19

Speak
for
Yourself

20

Language most shows a man; speak, that I may see thee.
—Ben Jonson

The man who said, "Monkeys very sensibly refrain from speech" was humorously pointing up one of the most important and distinctive attributes of man—his ability to communicate through language, through words. He was also emphasizing the great blessing and grave responsibility of possessing such an attribute, and that some of us could make better use of it!

"That's for sure," says a young person. "Sometimes I think that animals *are* smarter than people by not talking. Every time I open my mouth I seem to get into difficulty!"

Many of us don't know how to express ourselves effectively. But we can learn, and almost everyone understands how vital it is to our success and happiness that we *do* learn how to convey our thoughts clearly and correctly and convincingly.

Said Joseph Conrad, "Give me the right word and accent, and I will move the world." True, most of us are not anxious (or likely) to "move the world." We simply want to be able to speak with confidence and understandability. A good place to begin is to appreciate the *importance* of what we say and how we say it.

During World War II three Latter-day Saint boys serving in the Navy were invited for dinner in the home of a friendly family whose own son was overseas. As was their custom, the hostess served an alcoholic cocktail before dinner. One of the young men was confused and afraid to offend and hesitantly reached out for the glass. The second seemed insulted at the invitation (though the family knew nothing about the boys or their religious convictions) and indignantly refused the drink, embarrassing the lady. The third young man smiled warmly, graciously thanked her, and quietly explained that none of them used alcohol. During the course of the evening, *one* of the three was invited to teach the interested and responsive family the story of the gospel. It takes little imagination to guess which of them had this privilege.

Think of the power of words! With words we can bless or curse, criticize or praise, teach truth or falsehood. We can crush, sting, entice to evil, plant foul thoughts and unwholesome stories —or we can use words to inspire, encourage, show sympathy and compassion, share happiness. Words can be used for gossip, arousing a mob, injuring a good name—or to calm and comfort, counsel, teach faith, reprove, cry repentance. We can say yes, or no. We can mock and sneer, treat holy things lightly, "make man an offender for a word"—or we can worship and pray and forgive. With words we speak to our Heavenly Father and testify of his goodness and his love.

Words, then, are instruments. Their effect is determined by how, in what spirit, and for what purpose we use them.

To speak for oneself, with knowledge, using good judgment, knowing when to be silent; to leave unsaid the wrong thing at the tempting moment; to fit our conduct with our words—these are vital human opportunities; and there is something more. *We must be genuine.* Words may convey a message to the mind; sincerity sends a message to the heart.

We will probably never know how many parents have been brought to faith, how many schoolmates, neighbors, friends have come into the Church, how many servicemen have been baptized, because young Latter-day Saints knew enough about the gospel and had faith and courage enough to teach it and live it. What a marvelous harvest would occur if every young person in the Church were to learn the gospel and *speak for himself!*

In school, at work, at play, how important it is to be able to communicate clearly and live convincingly.

So,

In school, with your friends,
in seminary and committee meetings and the speech contest,
on your feet in testimony meeting and on your knees
in your room,
to the elderly and the sick and the suffering, the
lonely and frightened,
to your parents and family,
to the student who cheats or talks of it,
to your employer,

SPEAK FOR YOURSELF!

22

Hats Off to Youth

John Trebonious was a teacher in a German boys' school many years ago when schools were very formal and sometimes teachers were required to wear robes and hats (something like graduation outfits today) when they taught their classes. Professor Trebonious did not wear his hat in class and was asked to explain why he did not. He answered that he felt that he should keep his hat off in the presence of so many promising, excellent young men.

23

"Among those who sit before me," he said, "there may be some who will one day accomplish great things, lead nations, or even affect the history of the world. I take off my hat in respectfulness for what they are and what they may become." There was sitting at his feet as his pupil at that very time a little boy named Martin Luther, a boy who grew to great manhood and literally affected the history of mankind.

This is how I feel about you, the youth of the Church.

For though I don't know all about all of you, I know enough that is good about many of you to make me feel as John Trebonious did. I want to take off my hat to you.

I'm impressed with all that is good and strong and virtuous and loyal in you. I've observed that you want to do well; to be good for something; to be counted among the worthwhile and the accomplished. I pay tribute to your service, your spirituality, your scholarly interests, and your good sense of fun.

So, hats off to you, Youth!

I Am Ready for You

He wasn't sure where the idea had come from, but somehow the young man felt that if he could be alone in God's great outdoors and try to talk to his Heavenly Father, it would help. That's why he found himself standing in the grove of trees that early morning, looking up and saying what he did. His earthly father was not religiously inclined, and his mother had not forced the situation. The family therefore had had little formal religious experience or instruction, but the idea of praying for help had come to him, and he was trying.

24

His troubles were not abnormal, but they were serious. He had quit school and was associating with a group of companions who didn't really represent the kind of man he wanted to be. His work was unpromising, his habits questionable, and his future becoming more a concern to him daily. He really felt he needed some help, and he didn't know where to turn. Thus the idea of praying had occurred to him, and he had set out to do it, going outside his small western town to a nearby wooded area.

As he stood there that morning, the young man looked up and talked to the Lord. His message was simple, but to hear it as he described it several years later on an airplane flying over the jungles of Vietnam was electrifying.

"I just looked up," he explained softly, "and said to the Lord: *'God, I am ready for you if you are ready for me.'* "

There was no startling response, oral or visual. He saw nothing and heard no voice. There was only the utter quiet of the breezeless morning and the beating of his own heart. Yet he went away knowing that he had been heard, somehow deeply assured that the answer would be forthcoming.

When he sat behind the bus driver on his way to town that morning, he got the first phase of his answer. The man said to him, "Son, I believe you are looking for something that I can help you find." Thus started the conversation that ultimately resulted in the young man's acceptance of Jesus Christ and his restored Church, and that changed his life completely.

The corporal had discovered, when he was a sixteen-year-old boy, that God was ready for him. From that moment life had taken on a great meaning that activated him and exuded from him in goodness and strength as he walked and worked with humble dignity among his fellows.

Time for Good Balance

26

What do you think about when you hear the word *balance?* Do you get a picture of a performer on a tightrope, or you walking a pipe fence, or a ballet dancer on tiptoe?

These good and important and difficult young days—days of habit-forming, attitude-acquiring, decision-making—are the right days to think about balance, about wisely proportioning the different elements of our lives (as Christ did when he "increased in wisdom and stature, and in favour with God and man").

We all know someone who *isn't* very well-balanced, who isn't well-founded. MARTY MUSCLES may be long on weight lifting and short on friendliness or manners or studiousness or spiritual strength. PATTY PARTYGOER could seem to have a corner on cuteness and date popularity and be missing the talents and developed abilities a wife and homemaker must have to be successful. STEVE STUDIOUS might be wrapped up in books to the exclusion of experiences and associations that would help him to use his intellect to bring happiness to himself and mankind. Maybe RUTH RELIGIOUS fails to understand some of the most important principles of faith if she isn't serving and sharing and learning to love all mankind. It may even be that IRA INDIFFERENCE or DORA DIFFIDENT aren't taking time to develop their abilities in *any* of these pursuits, let alone seeking to balance their lives by working at *all* of them.

Isn't that the secret? One has to *take time, seek earnestly,* and *work* to get good balance in living!

Talents? Physical qualities? Circumstances? Different for each of us, to be sure! But time? The same number of hours each day for all of us! The desire and the willingness to work to develop our different abilities can be acquired. We have to *want* to be happy and useful and balanced.

So, take time to *study,* to read and think and prepare, to practice. Take time to *play,* to participate, to have fun and laugh. Take time to be *friendly,* to be interested and kind. Take time to be *healthy,* to walk and swim and bicycle, to eat wisely, sleep sufficiently, be clean. Take time to *learn manners* and to be mannerly, to listen, to express appreciation. Take time to *work* and earn your way, and maybe help out at home if this is your privilege. Take time to *serve,* to take part, to look around and be unselfish. Take time for *seminary* and sacrament meeting and home teaching or Primary teaching, and to visit the hospital or the lonely widow. Take time to *pray.*

There is time enough for all these things and more, but *no time to kill!* Many young people are doing things and finding *balance;* they are preparing for joy . . . and having it along the way.

27

Lincoln Kept on Growing

A truly great man was born on the twelfth day of February, long ago. He lived his boyhood days in a frontier cabin, and was denied substantially every blessing that most boys—even very poor boys—enjoy today. The preparations he made and the contributions that were his and the opportunities that came to him were all the result of an iron determination—and the will of God.

I am one who is prepared to believe that Abraham Lincoln was chosen by God and made ready by him in his own wise way for a great task that had to be done. I don't suggest that Abraham Lincoln knew it during those days of deprivation, but certainly there wasn't *any* mortal wise enough to suppose that much good could come of a boy condemned to such a birth under such circumstances, let alone to suppose that God was shaping a man to meet a challenge.

The early days of his manhood and maturity didn't look much like it, either. He was defeated again and again in his efforts to win political office and in other important objectives he established for himself. But he did not quit.

He was getting ready. Know it or not, he was getting ready. I remember the last lines of a great poem about Lincoln:

Lincoln was a tall pine.
Lincoln kept on growing.

That he had intimations that there were things he was to do seems evident. Long before he matched his steel with the dreadful problem of slavery, he said, "When I hit that thing, I'll hit it hard." And he just kept on growing.

Lincoln's heart was with the right and with the people. An old man who had listened to Abe at Gettysburg corrected the usual elocutionary presentation of his magnificent address there in one important particular: "Abe didn't say '*of* the people, *by* the people, *for* the people,' like they quote it," he said. "Abe said, 'of the *people,* by the *people,* for the *people.*'"

The right? It was Lincoln who said:

"I am not bound to win, but I am bound to be true; I am not bound to succeed, but I am bound to live by the light I have."

Think seriously about this man and what he was and did. We, too, are serving the right, and our chief concern is people— God's choice children. Keep serving and loving and growing.

Be Like Him

With his life Christ bought for us eternal life, if we are willing to accept it.

- In all worthy things he was the great exemplar
- He learned obedience
- He met the temptations of Satan
- He wept
- He sought a lonely place and prayed
- He loved and blessed little children
- He taught
- He forgave
- He encouraged the meek, the merciful, the poor in spirit, the pure in heart
- He made men hungry and thirsty for righteousness, and fed them
- He opened the eyes of the blind in body and spirit
- He rebuked and admonished and reproved
- He washed the feet of his disciples
- He met seeming disaster courageously, with faith
- All alone, feeling alone, he nobly paid the price for all men's sins. Not calling upon his "legions of angels," he willingly died the cruel death of the cross for us.
- In three days he rose from the tomb, was resurrected, and walked among men, blessing them
- He held out to us the gift of direction and inspiration for abundant lives here, and made possible for us eternal life.

But—" . . . what doth it profit a man if a gift is bestowed upon him, and he receive not the gift? Behold, he rejoices not in that which is given unto him, neither rejoices in him who is the giver of the gift." (D&C 88:33.)

Manners in Church

31

Scattered through the large congregation listening to the sermon were many young people. Two earnest young men had just reverently concluded their sacred service at the sacrament table, and a dozen boys had taken their seats after having carried the emblems of Christ's sacrifice to those in attendance. Testimonies of devotion and appreciation had been borne by two youthful speakers. All through the chapel there was intense quiet, and a spirit of reverence and worshipfulness.

All through the chapel except in one section, that is. Back in a corner a group of young people were paying attention only periodically and in between were whispering and leaning, looking at a book, writing on a paper and folding and passing it. The resulting disturbance, not severe enough to be offensive under other circumstances, reached every corner of the chapel. There were annoyed and accusing glances. For many, the spirit of worship was seriously impaired.

The fourth member of the group was a stalwart young man who sat quietly, reverently, trying to concentrate on what was being said. It was obvious that he was embarrassed by the thoughtlessness of the others who were not enjoying the wonderful spiritual experience they went to receive and might have had. Their disrespectfulness to others and their irreverence before God were unmannerly and ungracious.

Good manners do not mean courtliness or exaggerated acts of deference. Manners are a manifestation of good sense and good breeding and consideration for others. They are the "shadows of virtues. . . . " They are an outward expression of what we believe to be important, of our values. They reflect our attitude toward others; they show how we really feel.

"A gentleman's manners do not camouflage his character, but reflect it."

There are so many opportunities to show by our conduct how we feel about our Heavenly Father.

In participating in the Lord's Supper,
   in prayer, in service to his children,
      in teaching, in worshiping,
we express our feelings for him.

32

When we are reverent and respectful during some sacred appointment we are being mannerly in the best possible sense, and showing our love for him in a way that is pleasing and acceptable to our Father in heaven.

"Manners are the shadows of virtue . . ."
                    —Smith

Suitable behavior for sacred places includes:

lowering your voice, slowing your pace, stepping lightly

boys removing head covering

girls guarding against clicking high heels

dressing modestly, conservatively, inconspicuously

grooming carefully so that the breath is sweet and hands immaculately clean

smiling pleasantly, greeting members warmly

no boisterousness

no eating or chewing gum

no combing of hair

no clipping, cleaning, filing of nails

no repair of make-up, appraisal of dental work

no noisy or distracting actions

no knitting or rustling of papers

no cluttering

no wiggling and giggling

rather sitting quietly, atten-
tively, worshipfully

closing your eyes and bow-
ing your head during all
prayers
joining in an audible
"Amen."

Suitable salutations for:

Bishop . . . always Bishop
So-and-So
Counselor . . . Brother
So-and-So
Stake Presidency . . .
President So-and-So
Sunday School Presidency
. . . President So-and-So

General Authority . . .
Elder So-and-So or
Brother So-and-So

Women in positions of
leadership are referred
to as Sister So-and-So

33

The Gunship Leader

The whirling blades of a helicopter gunship don't provide much shade for a conversation in the sun, nor, for that matter, is the setting favorable for hearing one another. It was all the more puzzling that the young airman should be approaching his commanding officer just as the major was preparing to board his ship to lead his unit on a dangerous mission. As he thought about the incident later, Major Allen recalled that he may have sounded a bit impatient as he spoke to the obviously nervous young man.

"Well, what is it, Hobson?" he asked. "It's time to load up, you know."

"Yes sir, I know," the boy replied. "But . . . sir, I'd like to ask a question, if you don't mind."

The commanding officer's face softened as the crewman blurted out his urgent inquiry: "Me and some of the guys just wondered, sir, if you've had time to pray yet this morning."

"Yes, son," said Major Allen, very gently now. "I have had time to pray."

"Thank you very much, sir," he smiled, relieved. "We didn't want to start on this mission until you'd prayed."

Major Allen, former missionary, district president, faithful Latter-day Saint, pondered in his heart the implications of that

important question and testimony as he led another highly dangerous mission in the service of his country. The fact that the unit
had suffered many casualties without a fatality was widely known.
To the men in the group it had something very important to do
with their commander and his prayers. There had been no preach-
ing on the subject, only a keen sense of appreciation through the
unit for a commanding officer who led them fearlessly and very
skillfully in their dangerous work, and who had something special
about him that involved prayer.

35

Act for Yourself

I saw a very interesting thing occur the other night during a sacrament meeting. The person who offered the invocation at the meeting was short in stature. He bent the microphone arm down to fit his size as he prayed. We heard him well.

But then a very fascinating thing happened ! At first I thought it would occur once and then not again. But it did.

Every person who stood at the pulpit for the rest of the evening, most of them much taller than the individual who gave the opening prayer, either bent down (quite unnaturally) to that microphone or did not bend and was not heard by the congregation!

Not a single one adjusted it to his own size!

Can you imagine what I was thinking about for the rest of the evening?

What would you have been thinking?

My thoughts went to the scriptures, and to young people and their companions, and to human relationships in general. How many of us stay at mediocre levels because someone else "adjusted the microphone" for us at that height?

Surely we are uncomfortable there and unhappy and unproductive, but we do not change things: We let others set the standard for us. We march to their drumbeat, dance to their tune, follow their lead.

But the Lord said, through a great prophet: " . . . they have become free forever, . . . *to act for themselves and not to be acted upon,* . . . " (2 Nephi 2:26. Italics added.)

Decide for yourself! March to your *own* drumbeat! Set your *own* pace! And let it be the right decision, the steady drumbeat, the strong and enthusiastic pace. "Adjust the microphone" to the level where *you* can speak your own convictions, bear your testimony in strength, express your love, do your best. Refuse to let any other person set standards for you which are not worthy of you or of your high and noble calling or of the name you bear or the commission you have accepted.

God bless you to *act for yourself* and not be acted upon.

37

Will I Ever Forget?

38

QUESTION: I've been told that God will forgive and forget our mistakes if we sincerely repent? Will I ever be able to forgive myself and to forget?

ANSWER: The Lord has taught us that if we truly repent he will forgive our sins and remember them no more." Our forgiven transgressions "shall not be mentioned" unto us.

But there remains, in our restoration to wholeness, our need for the forgiveness of others and of ourselves.

Will we ever forget our sins? How can life ever be right if we continue to remember and suffer for our transgressions?

Alma knew about sorrowful memories—and he said a supremely significant thing to his son Corianton:

"And now, my son, I desire that ye should let these things trouble you no more, and only let your sins trouble you, with that trouble which shall bring you down unto repentance."
—Alma 42:29.

Corianton had committed a serious evil and had been sorely rebuked by his father. Alma's loving account of the atonement of Christ—his payment made in advance for our sins—humbled Corianton, and his father's good counsel set him on the path to restoration. But he still had his bad memories, and the problem of living with them.

Alma didn't promise that Corianton would forget. He taught him how to live with his memories, productively, humbly, continually appreciative for the mercy and long-suffering and forgiveness of God.

"You'll remember your sins," we can almost hear Alma saying. "You probably won't ever forget. But remember in the right way for the right reasons."

Don't let the sorrows that inevitably result from sin disqualify you from your blessings or your contribution. Don't shrivel inside when you hear the pointed sermon or lesson; don't turn from the brotherhood of the Saints or the path of the Lord because you've made mistakes. Don't give up and die, spiritually. Christ "suffered these things" that we might not eternally suffer, on condition of our repentance.

Let your memories "bring you down unto repentance"; let them "trouble you" only with that trouble which will keep you repentant. Remember—in order to keep fully alive the gratitude of your heart for the love of God and for what Christ has done for you.

39

Remember...in the right way for the right reasons.

Give Yourself for Christ

40

One of the most wonderful things about the Spirit of Christ is the feeling of helpfulness and friendliness and kindness that overcomes differences and makes men act like brothers.

It happened at his birth. There were rich people and poor people there, educated and uneducated, obscure and prominent. There were shepherds, tradesmen, stableboys, wise men, and angels. The spirit of that holy day brought them together in brotherhood.

Something very wonderful occurred on that sacred occasion: God's gift of his Beloved Son touched everyone round about.

The Spirit of Christ still makes us want to give, but some think they have little or nothing important to share. What do we have that we can give? What does the Lord want us to give?

In chapter 58 of Isaiah in the Old Testament, and chapter 25 of Matthew in the New Testament, we read of some precious things that every one of us has to give, if we will.

The Lord speaks of the *hungry* and *thirsty* and those who *need clothing* and invites us to "deal thy bread to the hungry," and "when thou seest the naked, cover him." He wants us to share the material things we have, and there is great need for this and great joy in it. But there is *more* than this. The poorest and humblest of us has gifts he can share. Think of these suggestions from the Bible:

"...SATISFY THE AFFLICTED SOUL..."

Are not loneliness and hopelessness afflictions of the most grievous kind? Each of us can help to satisfy this need. We can offer *friendship, interest, sympathy.* We can visit the sick and those who are alone. There are some who, more than anything else, would appreciate the gift of *thoughtfulness* and *attention,* of *compassion* and a little *time.*

"...BRING THE POOR THAT ARE CAST OUT TO THY HOUSE..."

41

One of the happiest holidays we ever had at our house (and the most joy to remember) was when a stranger in need was brought in to share our house. She complicated things a little and was a little "bother," but what joy she gave our children in accepting their love and affection! There are so many who are "poor" for lack of *kindness.* Is there anyone who has none of this to share?

"...UNDO THE HEAVY BURDENS...LET THE OPPRESSED GO FREE..."

Many who suffer from disappointments and separations and sorrow need nothing so much as encouragement and cheer. A prominent man once had a serious personal setback, and after a night of severe depression and distress, sat by his window as the sun rose, not knowing where to turn, heartsick and afraid. He heard a cheerful whistle and saw a figure passing by his window— the twisted figure of an old friend, a choice friend now tortured by the crippling effects of a tragic accident, a man who lacked many of the material things and advantages the watcher had. He turned from his window ashamed, but comforted and strengthened and resolute.

"...BREAK EVERY YOKE...LOOSE THE BANDS OF WICKEDNESS..."

The world suffers more for want of truth, knowledge, faith, than for want of bread. Have you a friend who lacks faith, who needs to know the program and promise of repentance? Pride, stubbornness, ignorance, unbelief, sin are terrible yokes for God's children to wear. Would a book or a letter or a word from you —a word of *faith, testimony, love, confidence*—be a valuable gift to them? Have you this to share? and the courage to do it?

Is there someone who has injured you and labors under the terrible burden of guilt and bad conscience? Would *forgiveness* be a good gift for him and for you?

"...HIDE NOT THYSELF FROM THINE OWN FLESH..."

A great man once said that young people should "not join a lot of gangs." "Join the United States," he said, "and join the family." There are those who love you best and who have done most for you who could not receive a more cherished gift from you than to know that you love them and *appreciate* them. If you've been "away," maybe, even living under the same roof in the same town, why not "join the family."

At Christ's birth, each gave what he had to the Lord. Whatever gifts you may have to give, will you consider how important it could be to others if you were to *give some of yourself* to them, in the spirit of Christ?

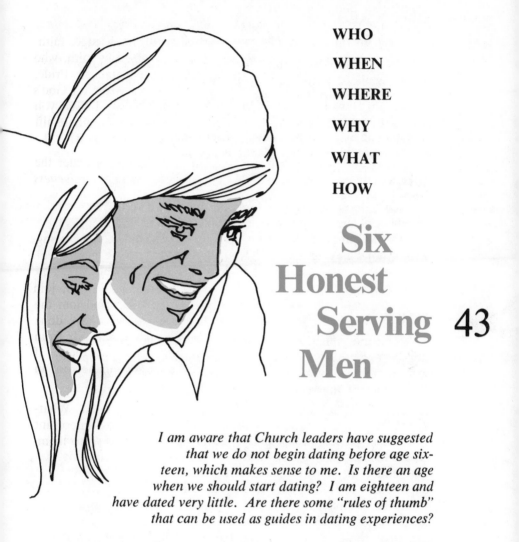

WHO
WHEN
WHERE
WHY
WHAT
HOW

Six Honest Serving Men 43

*I am aware that Church leaders have suggested
that we do not begin dating before age six-
teen, which makes sense to me. Is there an age
when we should start dating? I am eighteen and
have dated very little. Are there some "rules of thumb"
that can be used as guides in dating experiences?*

There are many choice statements as to the value and importance of learning to associate with others while we are young.
For instance, there is a quotation from President David O. McKay
in the book *Gospel Ideals,* under the heading, "The Importance
of Skills, Activities, Associations": *"The achievement of a happy
marriage begins in childhood and youth. The opportunity of marriage begins in the early days in school. The young girl who learns
to play the violin is more likely to find a good mate than one who
sits at home, refusing to go out in society.*

"The boy who participates in athletics is more likely to find a mate than one who sits by the radio. In other words, associations are conducive to happy marriages because one becomes acquainted, one with another. One has more opportunities for choice."

In this connection, think for a moment what the Church offers to its members, particularly to the young boys and girls.

As to so-called rules of thumb with reference to dating, one helpful possibility is to refer to Kipling's "six honest serving men" who taught him "all he knew." Their names are *What* and *Why* and *When*, and *How* and *Where* and *Who."*

WHO

Only those whose standards are high, like your own—strong members of the Church where possible. Several different persons, so that the purposes of courtship may be realized, neither going steady nor "playing the field," but getting to know a number of good people, broadening your associations and your objectives and your understanding.

WHEN

Not too young, not too often, not on school nights as a rule, not too expensively. When you really *want* to (at the proper age), and conditioned by when-you-*can* and when-you-*should* considerations. During the right hours; under the right circumstances.

WHERE

Clean places, decent places, proper places where you can be proud to be. Only clean movies or plays. No "adventuring" or "slumming" in dives or questionable surroundings. No place that parents or the Lord would not approve or where you and he/she would be ashamed to be found. No place where the Spirit of the Lord will not likely be present.

WHY

Associating with others under wholesome circumstances helps develop friendships and permits you to learn about qualities and characteristics in others, to get to know them, to have fun together, to widen areas of choice, to achieve a wider and wiser vision of what one may seek in an eternal companion, and to ultimately find someone who shares common convictions and character traits and whom you can marry in the right way in the right place by the right authority.

WHAT

Fun things, wholesome things, good and useful things. Church-going dates, work parties, service projects. Cultural and educational activities, close-to-the-beauties-of-nature experiences, hospital and shut-in visits, things pleasing to you, to parents, to God.

HOW

With others, in groups, chaperoned when proper, appropriately dressed, cheerfully, courteously, modestly, wisely, prayerfully. And let parents know where you are, with whom, doing what, and when you will return. Have a happy time!

45

The Knock at the Door

She was a vivacious, attractive young lady, and it was obvious as she spoke, an intelligent and earnest one. There was a tear in her eye and a deep intensity in her voice that made her question even more serious. "Why doesn't *everyone* join the Church?" she said. "If I could only pass on to others the great joy our family found through becoming members of the Church. . . . "

Her question is a good one. The gospel has been restored. The Church of Jesus Christ has again been organized on the earth. This is the truth, and both the Bible and Book of Mormon tell us that the Spirit of the Lord is given to every person to help him find the truth. Why, then, *doesn't* "everyone" join?

There are many reasons, including the very good one that many have not heard the wonderful story of the restoration; it is our responsibility to take it to them.

Another very important reason is that men are free to choose or reject the truth, to select "liberty and eternal life" or "captivity and death." All who *will* come to the Lord *may* come, but none is compelled to come. This Alma taught (Alma 42:27), and also that some deliberately, persistently choose to [*yield themselves*] *to become subjects to the devil.* (Alma 5:20.)

But happiness and truth come when a person *"yields to the enticings of the Holy Spirit,"* accepts Christ, and lives his commandments.

Thus each of us, whether we realize it or not, may and must choose his destination and his pathway. Every day we are choosing the road we travel on, sometimes failing to realize that we are at the same time choosing the place the road leads to.

God wants us to have freedom and happiness, but he will not force us. He wants us to have all that he has prepared for us and will give us all that we are "willing to receive," but he will not impose upon us blessings which we are "not willing to enjoy." (D&C 88:32, 33.)

Christ sends an invitation to each of us; he stands at the door and knocks. (Revelation 3:30.)

Every individual must decide whether or not he will listen to his voice and open the door to him.

47

Let there be many windows to your soul,
    that all the glory of the universe may beautify it.

From "Progress" by
Ella Wheeler Wilcox

Isn't it wonderful how many interesting things there are around to be seen and heard and felt and learned and enjoyed! Or have you noticed?

Lord Chesterton said, "There are no uninteresting things; there are only uninterested people."

Man is created with a soul to be fed, and with the urge to feed it. The needed sustenance is all around us, available. We have only to open the "many windows" to our soul—to happily employ our eyes and ears and intuition, to use our sense and our senses and our inward vision. We can furnish our minds with interesting pictures to look at, inspiring things we've heard, motivating thoughts we have read, happy memories to live with.

48  Many Windows

The great naturalist Dr. Louis Agassiz opened the door to an entirely changed life for a woman who complained that she had "never had a chance," when he asked her the composition of the glazed bricks in her dooryard upon which she rested her feet while she did her humdrum work. Her curiosity was aroused when she found that a glazed brick is vitrified kaolin and hydrous-aluminum silicate. When she had thoroughly investigated what that meant her written account of the search was published. Then Dr. Agassiz started her on an adventure to find out something about what was *under* the bricks in her dooryard, and her research on ants became an important book of 360 pages.

You can begin to open a few more windows and strengthen the most important development project in the world for you, your own soul!

Start now!

Ready for Inspection

The young marine was living proof of the adage that the eyes are the mirror of the soul. He didn't look much different from other men in "search and kill" units in Vietnam—until you saw his eyes. His uniform bore the marks of repeated exposure to the bush and the rice paddies; his face reflected that experience, too, and the anguish of four months on a hospital ship recovering from wounds. But the eyes were clear and unwavering, the effect of their steady gaze somehow touching and encouraging and conducive to confidence. It was startling how intensely the large group of military men listened as he spoke, following closely behind his commanding officer, who had just born his witness to the LDS servicemen assembled in conference at DaNang.

"Thank God for Major Elliott," said the boy. "Knowing him has helped me keep my life clean and sweet. I would like to tell you very humbly that I believe *my life will stand inspection.*"

What was it Paul wrote to the Corinthians?

"Let a man examine himself." (1 Corinthians 11:28.)

To so live that our lives will "stand inspection"—our own examination, the close observation of dearly loved ones and of other men, the loving, compassionate glance of the Lord—is to live with fulfillment and peace, even in the midst of tragic conflict.

50

Take a Lofty Look at Life

God has made all men to be happy. —Epictetus

Here is a tantalizing thought for a timorous teen in the magic month of May: BE HAPPY!

"Ah, yes," you say, "BE HAPPY! But how? What is happiness? Where is happiness?"

Happiness is at your fingertips. It is all around you. It is within you. Happiness is like the old man's spectacles which he cannot find. It is perching right there on the end of your nose, or sitting out of sight on your forehead, or there by your side at arm's reach.

Rudyard Kipling left a great thought. He said:

> *The best thing, I suppose,*
> *That a man can do for his land,*
> *Is the thing that lies under his nose,*
> *With the tools that lie under his hand.*

And so is the best thing one can do for his Church, his community, his neighborhood, his family, for himself. The scenes and seeds and sites of real joy or contribution or service are not in some far distant place or in some other circumstance. "Happy Valley" is not over the hill or down the road.

Would you be happy? Build firm foundations of faith. Look around you—at life, at the goodness in your fellowmen, at the graciousness of your Heavenly Father and the marvelous works of his creative hand and the inspiration of his high and holy purposes for you and all men.

Consider your present blessings. Which of them would you give up? How much would you yearn for them, and what would you do to get them if you did not have them?

Do your best at the task at hand. Plan and prepare for work to do that will be meaningful and congenial for you. Find happiness by loving and serving others, earnestly and unselfishly. Accept yourself as you are, but be your better self and move in the direction of your best self. Be wholesome. Be good. Make happy memories and cultivate a clear conscience by doing things that will be good to remember, and refraining from word and act and thought that will not be good to remember. Be courteous and kind and gentle to all. Insist on being happy. Said Abraham Lincoln, "No man is happy who does not think himself so."

You see! Happiness is within you and around you.

52

It lies under your hand.

God wants you to find it, enjoy it, and share it.

How Do You "C" Christmas?

Some young people were talking about the important "C's" of Christmas the other night. They came up with quite a list and tried to make them rhyme. No doubt you can think of some more. Here are some of theirs:

Children, candles, candy canes,
Cheer, (new) clothes, country lanes,
Carols, coasting, cranberries,
(Santa) Claus and chim-en-eys
Cards and cotton, colored lights,
Chocolate, church, and crispy nights.

It was fun thinking about the "C's" of Christmas (and slightly perverting the spelling of "chimney" to improve the rhythm), but real joy came when the conversation became more serious, and we talked with appreciation of the *most important* "C's" of Christmas—Christ and his loving *care* and *concern*.

The Savior cared very much about the five thousand who had to be fed and about the helpless man at the pool of Bethesda. He was concerned for the rich young ruler, for the woman who touched his robe, and for the children who wanted to be near him.

Mary Magdalene won his compassionate forgiveness, and Zacchaeus felt the warmth of his gracious heart and friendship.

So closely and lovingly was Christ identified with his fellow-men that when one of them suffered he suffered also; when one was helped or blessed, the good deed lifted him as well. When he talked of the end of the world, he said that certain ones would be on the right hand of the King, honored because they had served him and loved him and cared for his needs. Perplexed, not understanding, these "blessed" ones would gently protest his commendation, not remembering ever having ministered to him.

"Inasmuch as ye have done it unto one of the least of these my brethren," the King will say, "ye have done it unto me." (Matthew 25:40.)

Really caring about others, then, being unselfishly concerned with their well-being—these are the "C's" that represent the true spirit of Christ and of Christmas. These are Christ-like qualities. They are characteristics which we are here on earth to develop.

What better time and circumstance is there than at Christmas to show that we are learning genuine Christian concern, that we truly care about others?

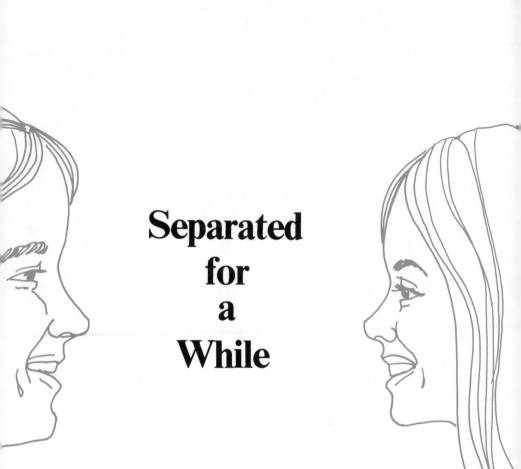

Separated
for
a
While

The young captain had volunteered for an extra period of duty in Vietnam, as had so many of his fellow servicemen, because he believed in the cause and was willing to serve it. His job as forward air controller involved flying a small airplane over the jungles and rice paddies looking for enemy activity. Often he found it when shots were aimed at him. He had survived many close calls in his assignment.

When he came to the meeting on this particular occasion, the captain had just finished flying another four-and-a-half-hour mission. He was obviously grateful to be able to be in attendance and to participate. He talked of his wonderful family at home and expressed appreciation that they were able to spend time together by means of tape recordings and letters. He talked of the sorrow of separation and of his great love for his family and of his confidence in them and in their growth and development while he was away.

As he spoke to us, our brother mentioned the sad example being given the local people by some American servicemen. "Let's show these wonderful Vietnamese people what true husbands and fathers are like," he said. "Let's give them a picture of honorable husbands and fathers as they should be."

His summation of the experience of separation from home and loved ones was sobering and compelling in its thoughtfulness:

"Those of us over here know what it means to be separated from our wives and children temporarily," he said. "We certainly don't intend to do anything that would separate us from them permanently."

56

This Life Is the Time

For behold, this life is the time for men to prepare to meet God; yea, behold the day of this life is the day for men to perform their labors.

—Amulek in Alma 34:32

Do any human beings ever realize life while they have it? Every, every minute?"

—Emily in *Our Town*, by Thornton Wilder

Where and when do you do any serious thinking?

Maybe it would be better to speak of what I mean as *solemn* thinking, when we ponder and consider what life is really all about and where we fit into the scheme of things. We seem to be able to do this best (maybe exclusively) when our hearts have been touched by some sweet spiritual emotion, sorrowful, joyful, or worshipful. At least, these are the times when we get the *right* answers, because then our hearts are humble, for the Spirit can speak only to a humble heart.

57

A group of us—young and older—did a little of this kind of thinking today at a funeral. The loved one being honored had lived a happy, full, productive life. She had been blessed with fine talents and had developed them and shared them unselfishly

with others. She had suffered severe pain and physical infirmity for many years but had served the community and Church and her choice family faithfully through it all.

Her children and grandchildren were there with loving friends at her funeral. This is one of the things that got me thinking solemnly. I wondered if the children understood the important things being said. I hoped they did and wished that other young people could hear also. One of the speakers mentioned some qualities which the children of this wonderful mother had received through her. He told us how hard she had worked and how much she had sacrificed to teach them and train them and to give them the blessings of a sound education, an acquaintance with beauty and truth, and a strong character. He said: *"Many people think that one grand lecture on how to behave should suffice, but this is not enough. It is not the way of a good teacher, and it is not the way of life."*

That is a great thought for young people to consider and for parents and teachers and leaders also. We don't "prepare to meet God" by listening to or delivering "one grand lecture" (or many of them), do we? It doesn't happen in an hour or a day. A wonderful lesson or sermon or conversation or book may help tremendously, but character isn't formed in a high moment of spiritual responsiveness or resolution. As the missionary Amulek told the Zoramites long ago, our preparation requires *performing, laboring.* It involves prayer and pain and patience, service and sacrifice, and a sense of responsibility. It includes learning and repenting and following through; it demands tears and trying, fulfilment, and some failure and frustration. It is living usefully now as well as preparing to live fruitfully in the future. It is meeting the "eternal everyday" with cheerfulness and courage and faith. It means learning to really care about God and our friends and family and others. It is as the poet said:

> *"Immortal life is something to be earned,*
> *By slow self-conquest, comradeship with Pain,*
> *And patient seeking after higher truths.*
> *We cannot follow our own wayward wills,*
> *And feed our baser appetites, and give*
> *Loose reign to foolish tempers year on year,*
> *And then cry: 'Lord, forgive me, I believe!'*
> *And straightway bathe in glory. Men must learn*
> *God's system is too grand a thing for that."*
>
> —Ella Wheeler Wilcox

Another speaker at the funeral helped us to think about the past and the future. He recalled the girlhood and school days of this lovely grandmother, speaking of her beauty and grace, of her ability in music and speech and the dance. (I sat wondering if her children and grandchildren had ever thought of her as having been young and vital and beautiful.) *"She was vivacious,"* he said, *"and she had the character which kept that vivacity within bounds. She had lots of fun within the standards of the gospel."*

This was the moment when I especially hoped that the grandchildren were able to understand, and I wished that all other vivacious girls and manly boys in the world could be there to hear and understand. Our faith and spiritual imagination were stimulated to permit us to look with the speaker to a future time of reunion when children and grandchildren again meet and associate with this sweet soul who had been in her youth a beautiful, vital, talented girl. She had lived her life well, he reminded us, and had made her preparation to meet God. Her descendants, "if they are willing to pay the small price of following her pattern, as she followed the pattern of the Master," will also be ready to meet God and their loved ones when this life is finished.

She was attractive and vital and popular—and *"she had the character which kept that vivacity within bounds!"* Because of this her life was wholesome and happy, and she passed on to her descendants a wonderful heritage and a glorious future.

This is where a brief period of "solemn" thinking took some of us today. Better than ever before we understood what Amulek was saying to the Zoramites. These people had forgotten the purpose of life. They were arrogant and selfish and self-centered. They were disobedient to the commandments of God. They were unkind, unthankful, impatient; they cared nothing for the well-being and happiness of their fellowmen. He was telling them that they must change, they must repent, and they must begin to do it *now, today, this hour.* *"This is the first hour of the rest of your life,"* he was telling them, *"and the first day."*

God wants you to change. He will help you. Christ died on a cross to give us the privilege of living eternally with God. If we are to have that blessing we must feel right about ourselves. Our "confidence must wax strong in the presence of God." (D&C 121:45.) We must prepare and labor in this life. The way is clear, the promise is marvelous, and *the time is now.*

Stretch Out

60

Summer is a great time for exercising the muscles and the imagination and for another kind of stretching out that some believe is the most difficult exercise known to man—that is, thinking, meditation.

Of course, this experience isn't limited to certain seasons or circumstances or places, but there is special magic in the quiet summer hour by the lake or the stream, or on the hillside, or in the forest or the field or the park.

What to think about or contemplate? Well, sometime you must think about and decide what kind of person you'd really like to be, what you want in a husband or wife, the family life you hope to have, the causes you will serve, the work you'll be happy doing, the kind of community in which you'd like to live. The possibilities for you are almost limitless, but one of the certainties of life is that you must limit yourself, you must choose.

Now is a good time to reflect on what you are and have, to think what you want, to consider what you must do to achieve your goals. Ponder your possibilities, dream some dreams, chart a course! Do your exercises! And remember what a wise man said: "Associate reverently, and as much as you can, with your loftiest thoughts."

Something Missing

"Suave politeness, temp'ring bigot zeal, Corrected 'I Believe' to 'one does feel.' "

—Knox

"I am convinced that a vague good will is not a satisfactory substitute for a personal philosophy that is the result of a hard, hammering testing and tempering process. Men need to have their values explicit . . . they need to be able to say 'I believe' and then to put into words what it is they believe."

—Teele

"Aggressive fighting for the right is the noblest sport this world affords."

—Theodore Roosevelt

Several years ago I visited an Arizona college campus during a "Religious Emphasis Week." My assignment was to speak at the opening student-faculty assembly on the theme of the week, which was "Something Missing." As I walked through the student union building just before the meeting, pondering the subject I was to discuss, I stopped before a bulletin board on which were listed announcements and advertisements by the students. One of them caught my eye. It read as follows:

FOR SALE
1929 Ford
Two Door Sedan
Nice Body and Fenders
NO ENGINE
$20.00
See Bob D.

I knew at once that I had the keynote for my talk on the theme "Something Missing!" This "for sale" automobile existed, it looked good compared with others of similar vintage and description, it seemed useful and desirable. But, in fact, it was neither useful nor valuable. It lacked the one indispensable element which could have given its existence real meaning. It had no motivating power. It was created to move, to function, to fulfil a purpose, but as it now stood it was failing to satisfy the reasons for its being.

We, too, have a reason for being. Our lives have meaning and infinite value to him who is our Eternal Father. We are important to our families and others, to our Church and communities and countries, to the world. There is purpose in our creation and our mortal experience.

How important it is to every one of us, young and old, to learn and accomplish the purposes of our lives, how vital that we fulfil the measure of our creation, how critical our need for strength and motivation and direction from the great Source of power. It is not enough to *look* good, to *seem* to be worthwhile, to sit idly by, to exist, when we could live and move and find joy doing work and giving service worthy of sons and daughters of God.

"Suave politeness," lacking conviction and courage, is not virtuous; a "vague goodwill" will not suffice the needs of mankind. Men are needed to whom conviction means more than comfort or convenience or acceptance by others. Before each human being is the challenge to learn the truth, to be able to communicate clearly and courageously what it is he believes, to live and act and think according to his convictions, and to serve loyally and aggressively in the fight for right.

To those who accept the challenge there will not be, here or hereafter, "Something Missing."

In Upper Rooms

It was unbearably hot outside, but worse inside. The brave, noisy strugglings of the two portable air conditioners only intensified the fact that everybody was suffering from the heat. The uniformed men and the civilians alike were soaking with perspiration, and the physical discomfort was sufficient to work against the success of many enterprises. Not so the meeting of LDS servicemen in the upper room of the barracks in Nha Trang.

More than two hundred men were crowded into the long, narrow room, all worshipful and expectant as they met with their visiting brethren from Hong Kong and Salt Lake City. As they were called upon, they responded intelligently and humbly and often emotionally. They spoke of their feelings for the Vietnamese and their determination to do their best to help those good people enjoy freedom and self-determination. They spoke of home and their families, of their pride in their brethren and other fellow workers. Gratitude for the Church and its organization and principles was repeatedly expressed. They thanked God for his help and for the comforting influence that prayer and faith in him brought them.

Physical discomfort was forgotten as men joined in prayer and hymns and in praising God.

When it was over I walked along the balcony of that building outside the upper room and thought to myself that this experience was not unworthy of the parallel to other meetings in "upper rooms" in other sacred places far away, some of them long ago. And then as I walked I saw a scene that sanctified the experience forever in my mind.

At the back of the room filled with young men greeting and speaking with each other and shaking hands and recalling experiences together, several uniformed men stood in a sort of human barrier, sequestering a small area where a matter of sacred significance was occurring. An officer was sitting on a chair, head bowed, while three men in flight uniforms stood in a circle around him with their hands on his head. All four were shedding tears as the three set apart their brother as a district missionary and gave him a blessing. Two of the three I recognized as men who had spoken of being on missions over enemy territory that very morning; the third was scheduled to depart on such a mission within the hour. The man in the chair was an officer of superior rank who was being given authority by the district presidency to perform a labor for the Lord.

It occurred to me as I felt the moisture in my own eyes that all the sermons I'd heard and all the experiences I'd had relating to priesthood could be movingly summarized in this sacred act of humble service in a small upper room of a barracks on a military base near the central highlands of South Vietnam.

The Most Important Thing in the World

If we were in a classroom talking about things that are important to every young person and someone asked, "What is the most important thing in the world?" what would you say? Would you say the gospel? or the Church? the priesthood? Very likely these answers would be offered. But someone in the room would very probably suggest that *the most important thing in the world is the individual child of God.*

And isn't this the answer? The gospel is God's plan to guide his children toward their highest possibilities here and hereafter. The Church is the institution or organization established on the earth through which individuals may participate and serve. The priesthood is the power God delegates to man to function in his name and officiate in the ordinances of the gospel.

65

The objective of them all is to bring about God's purposes for his children. In the Book of Mormon we read that the Lord created the earth for his children to live on. (1 Nephi 17:36.) The scriptures also teach us that his "work and glory" is to "bring to pass the immortality and eternal life of man." (Moses 1:39.)

Each individual is important also because of his influence in the lives of others. Most of us know of incidents where an act of courage by one person saved the life of another, or perhaps a number of others. In the Talmud is the statement,

"If you save one life it is like saving a whole nation."

This is literally true. I have often recalled the story of Sergeant Henry "Red" Irwin, a crew member aboard a B-29 Superfortress in World War II. High over the ocean on a bombing run, badly wounded, Irwin picked up a burning phosphorus bomb with his bare hands, struggled through the smoke and fire filling the airplane, had to stop and unlatch the navigator's table, and finally reached the pilot's compartment and threw the bomb out of the airplane into the ocean—a bomb that had exploded prematurely inside the plane and was burning at 1300 degrees Fahrenheit, 1,088 degrees hotter than boiling water! At the cost of tragic injuries that permanently disabled him and caused terrible agony, he saved the lives of eleven other men who because of his courage returned home to their families and occupations and opportunities.

Sergeant Irwin was a prayerful, deeply religious young man. The eleven men who lived because of him—and all of their descendants who live and will live because of him—owe their lives to the fact that long before the actual incident occurred Henry Irwin had built within himself the faith and strength and integrity upon which he relied when the moment of crisis came. He had decided in advance what he wanted and what he would do. He didn't have to stop and weigh the issues—there was no time. He acted, and with extreme courage, because he had prepared himself so to act when the time came.

Great physical courage is impressive, but there are other kinds of courage which bring results that are sometimes even more significant. Moral courage, the courage to be honest and honorable and virtuous in spite of pressures or temptations or circumstances, may require as much or more real strength and may have even greater consequences in the lives of others. The decisions you make now are important to your family, your friends, your community and country, and your Heavenly Father. And while it may seem quite far away to some of you, it should be said that you are also extremely important to those who will one day call you father or mother. The choices you make are in a sense their decisions, too, because they will be greatly affected by the course you set for them.

Are you making *wise* decisions? Are you making preparations for a happy, constructive adulthood?

If *you* are going to be ready to meet the marvelous challenge of this great new era of choice and change, you must recognize your limitations and your need for Almighty God. Reach out beyond yourself for spiritual strength. Learn the virtue of service and the holiness of prayer.

Fine young man or woman, take another look at yourself, at what you are and want to be and can be. Realize that this is a time of unequaled demand for physical and intellectual readiness, and for the spiritual and moral strength without which the rest is not enough. See yourself as important, purposeful participants in one of the most crucial and challenging times in history. Get the spirit of Theodore Roosevelt's great statement:

"Aggressive fighting for the right is the noblest sport this world affords."

Be happy! Get ready! Go to work!

Gifts You Can't Wrap

Robert Allen was a young man who was killed in a mountain climbing accident. His funeral was described by a young person who attended as a sorrowful but sublime experience, an occasion of introspection and rejoicing and edification, "one of the most marvelous experiences of my life." Sad as it was to lose such a choice young man in a world greatly needing his quality and character, the Spirit had born witness of God's wisdom and of his goodness and his love.

A young friend and companion spoke of the gifts Bob had given to him over the period of their association. They were beyond price to him.

Sharing

One was the gift of sharing and serving. Possessions, time, talents, knowledge, loyalty, concern—all were freely, graciously given. The sharing was of self—the manner of giving that affects and enriches lives. Few things bring such sweet satisfactions as the knowledge that we have a friend who really loves us, who really cares. God loves every one of his children—of that we are absolutely assured, we know it in our hearts—but God needs instruments of his love. He needs those who can carry his love and make it meaningful and personal in the lives of others. The shepherd's search for the lost sheep was a mission of grace and so was the joyful journey of the forgiving father when he ran to meet the penitent prodigal who had come to himself and had, with trepidation, started home.

Discipline

Discipline of self was another gift mentioned at the funeral—the example of a young man seeking and expressing self-mastery, self-direction, self-reliance. The two friends used to go to the university stadium daily and run up and down the stairs until they were exhausted, and they would try a few windsprints. Physical fitness was essential. Educational, cultural and spiritual challenges were approached with the same attitude and effort.

It was Mahatma Gandhi who said: "Even for life itself, we may not do certain things. There is only one course open to me: to die, but never to break my pledge. How can I control others if I cannot control myself?"

69

Excellence

Commitment to excellence was one of the gifts celebrated. It was to be sought in every endeavor. Bob went to the institute of religion nearby his school to practice the piano early every morning. He was entering medical school in the fall and felt he wouldn't have enough time to keep really sharp, and he wanted to do well.

To seek to achieve our best and improve it, to refuse a plausible second-level accomplishment below our possibilities, to be unwilling to settle for less than our strongest effort—this is to live with integrity and to supply a vitally needed example to others of a quest for excellence, whether in playing a piece, running a race, fulfilling an assignment, or representing the Lord.

Moroni referred to the "more excellent way."

"Wherefore, by faith was the law of Moses given. But in the gift of his Son hath God prepared a more excellent way; and it is by faith that it hath been fulfilled." (Ether 12:11.)

The gift of his Son made available the more excellent way, and in that way all of us can not only find a place, but can achieve.

Love

Love was the final gift mentioned and my mind turned to the newspaper account of a group of Christian missionaries in Ecuador who a few years ago were killed by members of a tribe they were trying to help and teach. They went to their deaths singing a great Christian hymn, the text of which is taken from 2 Chronicles 14:11: "We rest on thee, and in thy name we go." It has since been reported that the wives and families of those martyred men have returned to Ecuador to continue teaching the people of the same tribe.

Recently at a stake conference a young man was called to the pulpit with only a few moments' notice. He said he had been away to school and had come home to find a very dear friend in trouble. She had become enmeshed in the drug scene and had been tragically hurt. The young man sought the Lord in prayer, crying out for strength to help his friend.

He said: "For the first time in my life I truly forgot myself. While I prayed I came to a consciousness I had never before possessed. My concern for her was honest and intense and without self-reference, and I knew as I prayed that the love and concern of Almighty God for me and for my friend were pure and real and very personal."

Bob Allen loved his family and friends, the great people among whom he served as a missionary, the students from afar whom he befriended at school, and he loved the Lord. The inspiring account of this young man's life, given at his funeral, taught all present once again the real meaning of gifts and of giving, and that now is the time to begin.

The Perfect Law of Liberty

"Look, it's my life, and I'm going to live it. This is a free country, you know, and I'm a free man. What I do is my business and not the business of anyone else."

The youngster said it with a snarl and a sneer and with an intensity that made even the experienced counselor's blood run cold. He tried to talk with the boy about a "free country" and "free men" and whose "business" his serious moral misconduct really is. But the young visitor would have none of it. He was very sure of himself. He was "free" and intended to prove it by doing just what he pleased. This to him was freedom: doing just what he pleased, without thought or reference to anyone else.

When he had gone the counselor mused for a time about freedom.

Have you? Have you thought seriously about freedom?

Ask yourself, *What is freedom?*

How can it be obtained, and protected?

How much is it worth?

Who has it?

Is it the product of money, education, social prominence, political power, position?

What Is Freedom?

Often we think of freedom as absence of restraint on person or property or expression. We are "free" when we are outside prison walls, or out of debt, or are able to acquire and dispose of property, to manage our lives, or to meet together without limitation. We speak of freedom as the right and responsibility to make decisions—free agency. These precious "freedoms" the boy in the counselor's office is fortunate enough to enjoy. But there is a kind of freedom he does not have and does not understand, that has no political boundaries and nothing to do with dungeons or cells or lack of bread or opportunity. Sometimes it has burned particularly bright under just such conditions. It is the product of free agency properly used. It is the freedom spoken of by Jesus when he said,

> " . . . If ye continue in my word, then are ye my disciples indeed;
>
> "And ye shall know the truth, and the truth shall make you free.
>
> "They answered him, We be Abraham's seed, and were never in bondage to any man: how sayest thou, Ye shall be made free?
>
> "Jesus answered them, Verily, verily, I say unto you, Whosoever committeth sin is the servant of sin. . . .
>
> "If the Son therefore shall make you free, ye shall be free indeed." (John 8:31-34, 36.)

Freedom is a condition of mastery over *ignorance, unbelief, disobedience, unrighteousness.* He who escapes the bondage of sin is free.

How Is Freedom Obtained?

It is a gift of God through his Son to all who will receive it.

By learning truth.

> "And I will walk at liberty: for I seek thy precepts." (Psalm 119:45.)

By obeying the law.

"I, the Lord God, make you free, therefore ye are free indeed; and the law also maketh you free." (D&C 98:8.)

By accepting Christ.

"And under this head [Christ's] ye are made free, and there is no other head whereby ye can be made free. . . ." (Mosiah 5:8.)

By serving him faithfully.

"But whoso looketh into the perfect law of liberty, and continueth therein, he being not a forgetful hearer, but a doer of the work, this man shall be blessed in his deed." (James 1:25.)

By so living that we may have the Spirit of the Lord.

" . . . where the Spirit of the Lord is, there is liberty." (2 Corinthians 3:17.)

How Is Freedom Lost?

By uncleanness, unrighteousness, sin.

"Abide ye in the liberty wherewith ye are made free; entangle not yourselves in sin, but let your hands be clean, until the Lord comes." (D&C 88:86.)

To Give and to Get

Happy living involves generous measures of sharing and taking, offering and accepting. Giving and getting are both good and worthy experiences, the one requiring as much love, sincerity, and graciousness as the other. To know how to do both with grace and consideration is a mark of a mature gentleman or lady.

But our honest experience is that one is more real fun than the other!

74

Giving really is more genuine joy!

Sharing really is more satisfying!

IF THE GIFT GOES FROM THE HEART, WITH LOVE.

Sincere giving requires and develops love. They who love most give most, and they who give learn to love better.

Think of mothers, prophets, Christ, our Heavenly Father.

True, the receivers are not always responsive and gracious, but still those who love give.

Would YOU experience the joys of giving? Do you know where to start?

Serve God! Give him your heart!

> Christ has no hands but our hands
> To do his work today;
> He has no feet but our feet
> To lead men in his way;
> He has no tongues but our tongues
> To tell men how he died;
> He has no help but our help
> To bring them to his side.
>
> —Anon.

75

When we are fully ready to give God our hearts, we are ready to give him everything. He requires our hearts and our hands and tongues and time and strength. Serve the Lord in love. Give him your heart. Surrender your life to him.

There is a good first step available, right at hand. *Start in your own household* to honor God by respecting your family, and reach out to your neighbors. In small matters of personal relationships, be generous.

Giving our hearts, with love, is happiness.

Christian Brotherhood

There was an air of expectancy in the room. Several hundred Latter-day Saint servicemen had been permitted brief relief from action on the line to attend the Sunday morning religious services.

Those who had come early greeted each other and then sat quietly as visitors and local base officers entered the room. One of those in attendance was the base chaplain, a man of high rank and much experience. His courtesy in coming was beyond the call of duty. He had already arranged for the facility and had been most helpful in cooperating to make the meeting possible.

That he had come lent an extra flavor of graciousness and kindness, and those present were grateful. While not a member of the Church, he had been a good friend, and he was called upon to offer a few words of greeting. What he said amounted to far more than that.

"Good morning, my beloved brothers in Christ," he said, as he began. The spirit of his salutation and the sincerity of it and the strength of it touched every heart. Across the bounds of denomination or religious difference came the sweet, sensitive spirit of a devoted man, an earnest follower of Christ, speaking in the spirit of the Master he served.

As he finished, there came the united, reverent response of a large group of brothers in Christ who responded to his loving greeting with the solemn strength of their own "Amen."

We had seen and experienced the sweet blessing of brotherhood.

Help with the Monday Message

A wise man once said to a group of very young students: "No one is going to take you by your little hand and kiss the delight of learning into you."

Perhaps many present were too young to understand the full meaning of what was said, but most of them got at least the kernel of the suggestion: If you want to learn and to learn *how* to learn, you must do something about it yourself! You must pray for and cultivate the desire, and you must make the effort. No one can give another the "delight of learning." He can only lead him to it or provoke him to it.

There is another choice statement that applies: "Civilization will ultimately follow the course laid out for it by its youth."

That is, youth, growing older, will supply the answers as to what kind of civilization we shall have and in what direction it will move. It is vitally important, then, that young people learn in their youth the sound principles upon which society can be built and upon which alone civilization can survive. It is vitally important that young people accept this responsibility and begin early in their lives to exercise initiative in learning those principles.

Where and how shall this occur?

Church, of course, is one source, as wise, devoted, mature teachers and leaders help to guide and inspire. School is very important, and the neighborhood and community around us can contribute much. But the most important place to learn and apply correct principles is in the home.

The Church is putting increasing special emphasis on the home as a place of learning and living the great truths which make organized society possible. Constant emphasis is being placed throughout the whole Church on a Family Home Evening being held in each home each Monday. General Authorities and stake and ward leaders are encouraging all parents to hold this program in their homes every week.

This is where you come in!

You can't just wait for someone to somehow give you the "delight of learning." You can't just wait to see whether Mom and Dad are going to hold a family home evening on a regular basis. "Civilization" for you starts with the people you live with in your own home. How about helping things along? The twelve-year-old and the teen can have a mighty effect in getting this program functioning at home in the way it should, simply by wanting and asking for it. Few parents will resist very long a serious and sincere desire in their children for a really great family night.

So if your family is not holding home evening, prepare to get moving. Start talking about it. If you have family nights but only irregularly or on a poorly organized basis, get in there and help and plan. When the home teachers bring the manual to your house each year, you be the first to look through it and start planning for the happy experience.

Consider this promise made by the First Presidency to those families who faithfully hold their home evenings:

"Love at home and obedience to parents will increase. Faith will be developed in the hearts of the youth of Israel, and they will gain power to combat the evil influences and temptations which beset them."

I know that this is what you really need and want. So take the lead at your house in asking for the family home evening or in improving its quality and in starting to get the "delight of learning" that comes with understanding the most important truths in the world.

78

Light and Truth

79

We hear a lot about the activities of intelligent young men and women in the Church, and there are many equally intelligent whose activities go unrecorded. *What is intelligence? Is it important? How can it be acquired? How does it affect us? . . . .*

The scriptures teach that the "glory of God is intelligence," which is defined as "light and truth," or "the light of truth." The Lord said, "That which is of God is light. . . . " Intelligence, then, is light and truth and is of God. From the dictionary we get an interesting inkling of the nature of intelligence: the word comes from roots meaning "to gather or choose between." Intelligence is something infinitely more than an accumulation of facts or information, more than knowledge. It is the quality which permits individuals to choose from among many alternatives that which is good and wholesome, which is true, which is from God. It is the attribute missing from the character of Lucifer, who knew enough to be an "authority in the presence of God," but who lacked capacity to make wise choices. An intelligent person chooses to give his time and energy and allegiance to the things that count in terms of real human happiness and in serving the ultimate objectives of God. What is God's objective . . . his work and glory?

" . . . to bring to pass the immortality and eternal life of man." (Moses 1:39.)

To associate with our fellowmen in a way that lifts and blesses them, to develop our own capacity to serve God and his other children, to learn widely and deeply and to hearken to the counsels of God, this is to creatively co-operate with our Heavenly Father in accomplishing his holy purposes. This is to be intelligent.

Is it important to seek intelligence? How can it be developed?

"Whatever principle of intelligence we attain unto in this life, it will rise with us in the resurrection.

"And if a person gains more knowledge and intelligence in this life *through his diligence and obedience* than another, he will have so much the advantage in the world to come." (D&C 130: 18, 19. Italics added.)

" . . . seek . . . words of wisdom; seek learning *even by study and also by faith.*" (D&C 88:118.)

What is the effect of intelligence?

It is to enlighten minds, enlarge vision, clarify purpose, ennoble desires, strengthen resolve and will. It is to lead us to love God and obey his commandments, and to "forsake that evil one." (D&C 88:37.)

Young people, find ways to make school life—young life— happy and fruitful. For happiness comes, and satisfactions and success, through intelligent living—through lives which reflect truth and light in careful "gathering or choosing between," in high objectives, in a balanced program of wholesome activities and achievements and associations, in wide and wise interests and disciplined effort.

Preparation
for Marriage

EVERY NORMAL YOUNG MAN AND WOMAN wants (and should want) to get married—at the right time, under the right circumstances, to the right person. When the great occasion comes for you, you will want to be ready to be "the right person" for someone, and that takes more than dreaming! Every boy and girl, as they approach and enter the dating stage, should be aware that marriage is a great and demanding and richly rewarding challenge, requiring specific preparation if it is to be for them all that it can be and should be. Marriage has many aspects, among them these:

Economic

Providing for a family, and budgeting for and taking care of one, demands preparation, resourcefulness, discipline, frugality, dependability, and good hard work.

Cultural

Husbands and wives should be best friends, as well as sweethearts and companions. To be happy they must like being together and doing things together, or at least be mature enough to learn to like doing things together, and to be considerate and understanding of what the other enjoys.

Social or Emotional

This doesn't mean dancing divinely or going to parties, though the social graces are certainly important. It means that both persons must be grown up enough to be more interested in the success of the marriage and in the happiness of the other than in defending their own "rights." Married people who can't overcome selfishness and thoughtlessness aren't happy.

Romantic

High ideals, wise courtship, and the quiet conscience accompanying personal purity make a sound basis for the romantic relationships in marriage. People don't "fall" into love; they sometimes "fall" into something else. True love must be learned, achieved, climbed to; built on firm foundations of friendship, respect, consideration, kindness. Good manners and courtesy are vital, too.

Spiritual

When there is unity in religious interest, faith, and activity, marriage is inevitably happier. Around reverent search, prayer, worship, wholesome living, and religious service, fine family life can be organized.

In Season

My friend was speaking for the last time on this earth to a congregation of interested Church people, though neither he nor we knew it. It was wartime; he was a chaplain; and a few days later he lay dead on an island an ocean away from home. In that talk he quoted the poet: "Art is long," he said, and "life is fleeting." Some who were present remembered that night because it was his last with us. Others of us remember because of that— and because of the impact of his message:

Art is long, and life is fleeting.

One meaning of the message, of course, was that there is much that outlives mortal life, including man himself. Life is eternal, and because this is so, because the individual personality persists and always retains that which has been learned which is of eternal importance, one of the vital purposes of our earth experience is to discover and pursue that which outlasts it. Love endures, and honor and unselfishness and memory; every gain of the heart and mind and spirit continues with us forever.

There was further implication for me in my friend's message that night. Mortal life is fleeting and is vitally important as a proving and preparation period for the endless eternity of which it is part. Every age of man has its special blessings and opportunities and meanings, its pleasures and purposes. Each part of life has its own abundant harvests, but they are to be gathered in season. They cannot be rushed. Plucked early, the fruit is bitter and unsatisfying to the taste though it may look good and desirable; eaten, it may bring sickness and sorrow.

PLANTING TIME AND HARVEST

Someone has said:

"The flowers of all the tomorrows are in the seeds of today."

A fruitful life requires regular planting, and consistent producing, and the patience to wait. There is a time to be an infant, a time for childhood, for adolescence, and for adulthood. There must be a time for learning, for planning and preparation, for apprenticeship and useful work, for making friendships, and for dating and dancing. There is a time to acquire skill at cooking and sewing and music, a time for marriage and a family. There is a time for learning reverence and prayer, and a time to learn play and wholesome recreation. If the harvests are to be happy, there must be planting and nourishing and nurturing, cultivating and caring, and a suitable growing season and climate. Attempting to rush into what an expert called "half-baked adulthood" is foolish and often tragic. We cannot violate the program of nature; without suitable planting there will be no desirable harvest.

"AS FOR YEARS"

In 1831 the Church was moving West. A group recently arrived at Thompson, Ohio, earnestly desired guidance from the Lord as to how long they would stay there, and what they should do. The answer from the Lord was marvelous, applicable to all men in all times, everywhere. He said,

" . . . I consecrate unto them this land for a little season, until I, the Lord, shall provide for them otherwise, and command them to go hence;

"And the hour and the day is not given unto them, wherefore let them act upon this land as for years, and this shall turn unto them for their good."

—D&C 51:16-17

84

The lesson for our times? (All men need to know it): Work where you are as if you would always be there. Live in a rented home as if it were your own, tend the lawn, clean the wallpaper. Notwithstanding the uncertainties of your future, study your lessons; guard your moral standards, your character, your reputation; do your work with an eye to returning. Live and work and learn and act where you are "as for years," and you'll always be welcomed back; there will always be harvests to be gathered IN SEASON.

Art is long, and mortal life is fleeting, but eternity is endless, personality persists, and the joy of a bountiful gathering will always be his who takes life a step at a time, learning and living, planning and enjoying, planting and harvesting.

Year-round Values

January

Constancy and Fidelity

"But last year I earned my fourth individual award," the girl in trouble reminded her bishop.

"What will my fellow Scouters say if they learn about this?" worried the Eagle Scout caught in a car "borrowing" spree.

"Remember that I've worked after school for you for three years, sir, and never taken any money before," the young clerk suggested remorsefully.

"I've never lied to you until now, Dad, but I was afraid you wouldn't understand this time," cried the student after a late date.

To youth swathed in the circumstances that new experiences permit, it is most helpful to pointedly remember childhood teachings of truth even though parents and teachers may no longer be on every scene to pat heads, to caution, to comfort, to remind. There is no time, no situation, when truth doesn't apply. Once-in-a-while-ness or just-this-once kind of thinking have taken many a fine boy or girl down the slide to a pitiful kind of playground. The devil's territory is inhabited with people who "didn't mean to" or "weren't aware of consequences" or who "went along with the crowd just this once" or who "had never done it before."

Richard L. Evans has taught us that "occasional dependability isn't a dependable dependability and reputations made by many worthy acts are often lost by a single unworthy one."

The scriptures repeatedly urge us to endure to the end, to be faithful until the day of our salvation, to cleave unto the Lord and his teachings—all of this that we may know fulfilment, all the joy there is now and in the life to come.

February

Sincerity 87

If you can't be a pine on the top of the hill
Be a scrub in the valley—but be
The best little scrub by the side of the rill;
Be a bush if you can't be a tree.

This little verse by Douglas Malloch has been memorized down through the years by countless boys and girls who have been motivated by it to be what they ought to be, be what they want to be, be what only they can be. Perhaps it will put a burr in your back to do the same.

Playing the role, being a phony, copy-catting a friend, aping another, are painful substitutes for the real you. They are, in fact, a kind of immorality. Marcus Aurelius said: "This is moral perfection: to live each day as though it were the last, to be tranquil, sincere, yet not indifferent to one's fate."

It is pure joy to be in the company of someone who looks for the good in others and shares the knowledge of it—sincerely. It is inspiring to mingle with those who are unaffected, genuine, who have a creed and live up to it earnestly. "To be what thou seemst!" to have honesty of intent, to be openhearted before God and man is to know real peace of mind.

March

Wisdom and Bravery

What was it the good man said? . . .

> *"Deign on the passing world to turn thine eyes,*
> *And pause awhile from learning and be wise!"*

It is important to learn about the world; it is more important to learn what the world is about. The one pursuit leads to knowledge, the other to wisdom.

To be wise is to combine truth and virtue, to know that we must have something to live for as well as to live on, to realize that there are causes bigger than and beyond ourselves which we are here to discover and to serve. Wisdom persuades us to turn away from the things that matter least and to give our love and strength to the causes that matter most.

What are the "things that matter most"?

Addison said that the *"wise man is happy when he gains his own approbation, and the fool when he recommends himself to the applause of those about him."* To have the approval of one's own conscience is a supremely important thing. No other success is in any degree comparably satisfying. Wisdom is knowing this.

From Wordsworth we are reminded that *"wisdom is often nearer when we stoop than when we soar"* ("The Excursion"). To love God and to trust in him matters very much. To recognize our limitations and great needs and to learn to seek him and to look to him for help is wisdom. Asa of old learned wisdom: *"We rest on thee, and in thy name we go."* (2 Chronicles 14:11.)

Our country matters, our families matter; it matters that we prepare thoroughly to serve both. To love mankind, to accept others as they are and to help them and lift them, to respect their minds and their individuality and their integrity, this matters.

Wisdom is knowing which things matter most and serving them courageously.

88

Innocence and Repentance

Every one of us needs repentance, since each of us has fallen short of our own ideals and aspirations and of the contribution and conduct which should have characterized our lives.

Repentance, as we know, is more than an act; it is a program of construction, of reconstruction, of growth. It is a principle in God's plan for us which permits us to recapture a lost sense of innocence and wholeness and acceptability.

Most of us have learned something about the steps involved in true repentance. Look honestly at some matters in which it would be well for us to maintain our innocence or to regain it through genuine repentance:

(Mark carefully in your minds and hearts the words of Proverbs 6:16-19:)

"These six things doth the Lord hate: yea, seven are an abomination unto him:

89

"A proud look, a lying tongue, and hands that shed innocent blood,

"An heart that deviseth wicked imaginations, feet that be swift in running to mischief,

"A false witness that speaketh lies, and he that soweth discord among brethren."

Pray God that none of us will be guilty of shedding "innocent blood," one of the sins abominated by the Lord. But what of the other "six things"? Are we innocent of these? If not we should repent, and quickly. Then we may feel more consistently able to keep ourselves innocent of the other sins of the world which can destroy us and disqualify us from our blessings. Then we can with confidence repent and grow strong in the Lord.

Happiness

Happiness to a girl (especially an LDS girl who understands God's plan) means having spring in her heart all year long. It is loving and being loved. It is, ultimately, a temple marriage and a home blessed by the power of the priesthood, with children to bring up unto God. Happiness is fulfilling the measure of her creation.

To an LDS boy it is much the same. For one without the other is incomplete, and full joy, greatest glory, are limited. To be happy is to be part of the partnership with God someday.

And that's what dating is really all about!

There are those who would announce that dating is just for fun, a segment of youth, a trend of our times, a plague upon parents, and big business for the entertainment world. But to those who care about this precious span of life, who yearn for the *all* of it, dating is not an end in itself. It's a needful part of the plan —mingling, to know and be known, to then settle for one and be sealed for time and all eternity. Someone has said, "When the one man loves the one woman and the one woman loves the one man, the very angels leave heaven and come and sit in that house and sing for joy."

90

That's how it ought to be. That's how it can be.

But first one must appeal to another. It isn't enough to be good. Many a "good" person has been brushed aside for a more exciting-looking one.

It isn't enough merely to look sparkling or current, to be cleverly "with it." There must be something within to back up external attractiveness, to give quality to the relationship.

Ben Franklin's reminder, *"If you wish to be loved, be lovable,"* should be inscribed across the heart of every boy and girl whatever his or her age. It is the secret to social success, to satisfying companionship, and to happy marriage. It has everything to do with making the most out of what you have to work with in appearance, talents, personality, and spiritual inclinations. It is another way of saying, "Do unto others as you would have others do unto you."

Such a system of personal relationships shouldn't end with the altar, of course. Happiness, to be enduring, must be assured by continuing delightful associations and experiences with each other. In marriage (or even in dating) there should be a conscious effort on the part of each person to be worthy of the attention and concern of another and to be worthy of being loved.

"Most folks are about as happy as they make up their minds to be," according to Abraham Lincoln. LDS youth with an eye to eternity should make up their minds to be happy, to live happily.

June
Health and Long Life

It takes more than a wish to insure health, wealth, and a long life on this earth. This anybody knows. There are certain disciplines, however, that can aid the fulfilment.

The body is the temple of the spirit. The thrust toward perfection is power we put forth in bringing the physical into blend with the spiritual. Today is the time to perfect the body, the mind, to develop the senses and control the passions. Consider this writing by Thomas H. Huxley:

> "That man [is educated] who has been so trained in youth that his body is the ready servant of his will, and does with ease and pleasure all the work that, as a mechanism, it is capable of; whose intellect is a clear, cold, logic engine, with all its parts of equal strength, and in smooth working order; ready, like a steam engine, to be turned to any kind of work, and spin the gossamers as well as forge the anchors of the mind; whose mind is stored with a knowledge of the great and fundamental truths of Nature and of the laws of her operations; one who, no stunted ascetic, is full of life and fire, but whose passions are trained to come to heel by a vigorous will, the servant of a tender conscience; who has learned to love all beauty, whether of Nature or of art, to hate all vileness, and to respect others as himself."

91

To abstain from strong drinks, tobacco, and hot drinks, to eat in moderation wholesome foods, with thanksgiving, is a blessed bit of wisdom the Lord revealed to his children through the Prophet Joseph Smith nearly 150 years ago. To those who keep this commandment comes a promise that they

> *"shall find wisdom and great treasures of knowledge, even hidden treasures;*
>
> *"And shall run and not be weary, and shall walk and not faint.*

*"And I, the Lord, give unto them a promise, that
the destroying angel shall pass by them, as the children
of Israel, and not slay them. Amen."* (D&C 89:19-21.)

July

Freedom from Doubt-Anxiety

Faith is a pure mind, knowing of God and our relationship
with him and to him.

Faith is freedom from doubt and anxiety. It enlarges our
soul, quickens our mind, purifies our heart. Without faith nothing
can be accomplished. With it all things are possible. Reading all
of Alma 32 in the Book of Mormon is a thrilling lesson in faith.

Faith laughs and lifts in the face of fear or threat. To
believe is to be powerful. To be troubled with doubts, to turn
away from God, not to believe that he knows and loves each
of his children, is to suffer needlessly. The Lord has told us to
*"believe in God; believe that he is, and that he created all things,
both in heaven and in earth; . . . believe that man doth not comprehend all the things which the Lord can comprehend."* (Mosiah 4:9.) Knowing this, believing this, we should be like Victor
Hugo's bird *"who, halting in his flight on a limb too slight, feels
it give way beneath him yet sings, knowing he has wings!"*

Learning to live with uncertainty is part of growing up.
Youth faces the future knowing it is there (while age wonders
where it has gone), but is rightfully concerned with decisions
and questionings about what must be done with it. One can never
be sure, not even a young one, of what tomorrow will bring. So
today must be lived on the limb, with confidence in right doing,
in best efforts, in strides down the path in the direction God sets.
Then come what may, the song, the song!

The world is wide
In time and tide,
And—God is guide;
Then do not hurry.
That man is blest
Who does his best
And leaves the rest;
Then do not worry.
Charles F. Deems, "Worry"

August

Marriage

Are you looking to a future of "conjugal felicity"? What's that, anyway?

Why, that's a different and interesting way to say "happy marriage!"

It isn't likely that many of us will find much occasion to use the phrase, but all of us are interested in what it means and how to achieve it. " . . . *marriage,*" we know, *"is ordained of God unto man"* (D&C 49:15), and happy marriage is the only kind any of us wants or is looking for.

How can one be sure of a happy marriage?

By being prepared to give happiness to a beloved mate— and by finding "that someone" to marry who is prepared to provide a climate and circumstance in which you can be happy.

Sounds simple! . . . but is it?

No!

93

Marriage is the most choice and rewarding . . . and challenging and difficult . . . of human associations. It is an *"enterprise for mature adults,"* someone said. Of course, maturity isn't necessarily tied to calendar age, but experience demonstrates clearly that teens aren't usually mature enough to be happily married. We should start thinking *about* marriage early (so we can be preparing for when the time comes), but we shouldn't think *of* marriage until we are maturely prepared enough to be married . . . and have grown to love a partner who is also prepared.

Are you ready to be a wife and mother and the heart of a home? Or a husband and father and the head of a home?

Do you realize that physical attraction and affection are important primarily as *expressions* of the character and common convictions and respect upon which real love (and happy marriage) must be based?

Marriages fail when love is "too little." "Conjugal felicity" depends upon our having learned to love wisely and well, deeply and sincerely and unselfishly.

Healthy Mind

All of us are interested in having and keeping a sound, healthy mind—and in understanding how to achieve such a blessing.

The apostle Paul told young Timothy that he must not be ashamed of the testimony of the Lord or of his servants. *"For,"* wrote Paul, *"God hath not given us the spirit of fear; but of power, and of love, and of a sound mind."* (See 2 Timothy 1:7-8.)

Yet one of the chief enemies of a sound mind is fear—fear of ourselves, fear of others, fear of the future. We are afraid that we are not loved, or not worth loving, afraid that we are unworthy or unimportant to God, or that we have disqualified ourselves from his forgiveness or his concern. We get apprehensive about the future and our ability to live in it successfully; we fear our doubts and our doubting. All of us have known fear and thus know the force of fear to disquiet and upset our minds. What shall we do with it?

The "spirit of fear" is not of God. This "disease of the mind" is vulnerable to faith and cannot persist where there is true understanding of God and trust in him. "I will fear no evil," said the Psalmist: "for thou art with me; thy rod and thy staff they comfort me." (Psalm 23:4.)

There is a parable that begins: "Fear knocked at the door. Faith answered. No one was there."

To help settle our fears we need to be reminded that God loves us and others love us. Earnest effort and preparation banish insecurity: " . . . if ye are prepared ye shall not fear." (D&C 38:30.)

The problem of bad conscience can be overcome with sincere repentance and a willingness to accept the mercy of God. Most of what we fear of the future will never happen; what does happen we can endure, with the help of God. No one of us can carry all of the anticipated burdens of all the tomorrows, and none of us should try.

We must not permit our doubts to rule our lives. "Our doubts are traitors" (Shakespeare); faith and trust are loyal friends. Their presence assures a healthy mind.

94

October

Hope and Trust

There were two buckets sitting on the edge of a well. One turned to the other with mouth drooping down and said, "All I do is go down and come up and go down and come up all day long. No matter how many times I go down and come up, I always go down empty." The other little bucket smiled brightly, "That's funny. I have the same task. All I do is go down and come up and go down and come up all day long. But no matter how many times I go down and come up, I always come up full."

That's positive thinking. Hope is positive thinking. Hopeful people are happy people who take the changes and chances of life in their stride, worrying not so much about what happens to them as what they do about it. They look for the best in people and make haste to be kind, to help, to appreciate.

Samuel Smiles suggests that the best kind of self-help in the area of building hope in the soul is to consider that "hope is like the sun, which, as we journey towards it, casts the shadow of our burden behind us." This too will pass, the scriptures say, and that goes for the delightful moments as well as the trying ones. Hope sweetens the memory of experiences well loved. It tempers our troubles to our growth and strength. It befriends us in dark hours, excites us in bright ones. It lends promise to the future and purpose to the past. It turns discouragement to determination.

To have hope is to believe in God, to be grateful to him for a chance to live life, to be part of the plan, to be of service to him. "All that I have seen teaches me to trust the Creator for all I have not seen," said Emerson. He is there waiting to bless us with all we will accept. It is up to us to be in love with life and with the best way of living it: "buckets" coming up full and not going down empty.

November

Success

No one has success unless he abounds in life . . . in the getting up each day with a thirst for the challenges thereof . . . in the thrilling at the beauty of the world . . . in the love of people . . . and a closeness with God . . . in filling his niche by working at his task—whether it is rescuing a team from defeat or a soul from the depths.

Success needn't be a far-off thing, something reserved for old age, the rich, the wildly busy, the power structure in your place. Success in life has to do with what one *is* at any given time. It is a state of being rather than becoming.

> *Tomorrow's fate, though thou be wise,*
> *Thou canst not tell nor yet surmise;*
> *Pass, therefore, not today in vain,*
> *For it will never come again.*

This rhyme encourages action at this moment, and it is upon this fact that we'll be judged as a success or a failure. The successful person of any age is the one who rises to the occasion with his or her best efforts. What a blessing to a group, a school, a church, a community is the person who cares enough to contribute. Such success is based on the doing not the talking about it.

What can be done by one young? The same as by one older . . . *something* and done well. It may take a different form (like a system to upgrade teenage behavior instead of founding a bank), but it has a place, fills a need, marks success. Youth can stand firm amid teasings and tauntings; rise early and spend the hours carefully; give big meanings to principles and small importance to temporary pleasure; think creatively about wholesome ways to have fun, to mingle or single, to serve, to mutually improve.

Success is simply doing what you ought to do when you ought to do it in the best way it possibly can be done. It is total commitment to an effort—whether it's chairmaning a dance or overcoming a fault. It's learning to know God and putting a hand in his. It is looking at disappointment or the defeat of the moment with a wry smile and getting on with the business of growing, of being, of doing—better than before.

December
True Friends

Does anyone need to be taught the value of good, true friends? It would hardly seem so, since few of life's blessings are so clearly important. But all of us need to be reminded occasionally, and all will profit from a few moments' consideration of their worth.

The friends thou hast, and their adoption tried,
Grapple them to thy soul with hoops of steel.

Thus Shakespeare saluted the virtue of loyal, tested friends—and stressed the importance of retaining them.

How can one make friends and keep them?

To find a friend, be one!

Do kindnesses for others. Think of them, serve them, share with them.

Have happy times with others. Talk together of pleasant things, and problems, and deep things, too, at the level of your own understanding. Jest a little, and learn to differ without rancor.

Keep the confidences of others. Let them feel that they can speak freely, knowing that you will accept their offerings faithfully, keep the grain, and "with the breath of kindness" blow the chaff away. Shelter no unkind word or misunderstanding in a corner of your mind to harden and enlarge and emerge again in a moment of tension to hurt and destroy.

97

"Go often to the house of thy friend, for weeds choke the unused path."

Be impatient with separations, and welcome with joy your reunions.

Accept affection from your friends, and give it. Appreciate them, and let them know. Laugh with them often, and sometimes weep with them. Rely on them. Be true to them.

And let all you would give to any other friend be given to those who live in the same house with you, and to your Heavenly Friend, for these should be your closest and best friends of all.

This Is Your Church

The trip from Palmyra to Payson or Pasadena or Portsmouth or Perth—or wherever you are—is a long journey historically. What was behind it all? What is there in the Church for your generation?

Its Principles

98

The Church is built on eternal principles of truth, truth about God, Christ, life, and man.

God is the Father of the spirits of all men. He is the living, revealing, personal Father of whom the prophets spoke and whom they represented. He is the Loving God to whom Jesus taught us to pray after this manner, "Our Father who art in heaven." He is our Heavenly Father in whose image and likeness we are created, who loves us and reveals his will through his prophets.

Jesus Christ is the divine Son of God, the Savior of the world, our personal Savior. He is what he said he is, "the truth, and the life." He is more than a master teacher or ethical philosopher, he is the Redeemer, the Son of the Living God.

Life is purposeful and meaningful. It is not a "veil of tears" which we endure bravely. It is not a playground where we fritter away our time, indulging appetite and following after carnal or material desires. It is a schoolground, a testing place, a preparation experience, a "mortal probation" in which we are supposed to be learning the lessons which will equip us for eternal creative service with God. Virtue is priceless. Marriage is a sacred eternal covenant between man, woman, and God. When made under the law and authority of God and preserved in righteousness, marriage endures beyond the grave. Families are eternal units. We take with us through the door called death not the things we can count, but the things that count, the gains we have made in mind and heart and spirit. Life is good and purposeful, and goes on forever.

Man also is good. Because he is mortal and physical, he is subject to the temptations of the flesh. He is a free agent, and he lives in a world where the forces of evil tempt and mislead. But man is more than flesh, he is spirit, and his spirit is the offspring of Almighty God. He is therefore susceptible to the enticings of the Holy Spirit. He has within him the "upward reach." He is free, eternal, creative, brother to all men. He has the capacity to choose, and the responsibility to answer one day for the choices he has made. Man is meant to grow, and he grows as he learns to conquer that which is earthy in him by listening to the whisperings of the Spirit. Man is a child of God; he is meant to learn to be like his Father.

Its Organization

The Bible teaches that Christ grew "in wisdom and stature, and in favour with God and man." Each of us should also be constantly seeking to strengthen our relationship with our Heavenly Father and with our fellowmen, and to increase in intelligence and maturity and physical well-being. Willing individuals can most effectively grow and serve and contribute when their efforts are organized, and *in the Church are found the programs through which all of this may be accomplished.*

Priesthood quorums are organized in which every male twelve years of age and older is enrolled. Study, service, and brotherhood make these quorums great foundations for the personal well-being of individuals and families. Knowing that "the glory of God is intelligence," the Church encourages learning in every wholesome field, sponsors universities, and provides seminaries and institutes of religion near high schools and non-Church universities to insure opportunities for religious education and spiritual growth. Primary and Sunday School and Aaronic Priesthood MIA have full programs of activity for children and youth. Single adults eighteen years of age and older find special service, activity, and spiritual opportunities in Melchizedek Priesthood MIA. The women's Relief Society channels charitable services and includes programs for growth in homemaking skills and in educational and cultural as well as spiritual fields; the welfare program meets the needs of every participating member in a time of difficulty.

In dancing and drama, in athletics and music and public speaking, in youth leadership and health education and the development of social graces, in missionary work and temple service, the Church provides organized and well-led programs designed to bless individuals with opportunities for maximum effectiveness in participation and leadership.

Its Authority

The ultimate source of the laws and standards by which man is governed and by which he ultimately will be judged is God. Man is free to choose; he may obey or disobey eternal law, but he cannot himself change or "break" God's laws; he can only "break himself on them," if he insists. Not societies nor nature nor humanity can be set up as the origin or arbiter of eternal truth; God alone serves that function. The task for men is to work out a suitable balance between initiative and integrity and individuality, and the humility to accept the will of God and the leadership of his appointed servants.

100   The Church has received the divine commission of God to serve his holy purposes. It is led by men who have been commissioned of God to represent him. In it every worthy boy and man can be given the authority to speak and act and work in the name of Almighty God. This is an awesome commission and the most sacred of trusts. It is to be experienced by those who prepare themselves to have it and who will honor it. It is to be executed by those with "clean hands and a pure heart," who will be worthy to be the Lord's agents and to perform his errands.

Its Growth Through Participation

The organization of the Church not alone permits but demands participation of its members. There is no professional ministry, no compensated clergy to carry the load of service and leadership. As in the days of the Savior, ordinary men who work at ordinary human pursuits are called to positions of extraordinary importance; they become missionaries, teachers, bishops, stake and mission presidents, and apostles. Men grow through responsibility and participation and creative expression—and men came to this earth to grow. So farmers and doctors and salesmen and craftsmen earn their bread for self and family, and serve the Lord for the love of the labor. In the Church everyone who will participate is given opportunity, and everyone is encouraged to participate.

Young and old take part and learn to follow and to lead. All of the priesthood quorums and auxiliary organizations are officered and taught by members, and the great recreational, cultural, welfare, and spiritual programs are so conducted.

So the Church means *unselfish service*. *It imposes an obligation* and *provides an opportunity*. *It demands something and offers creative activity and achievement*. *It requires sacrifice and brings development and growth toward godliness*.

Its Theology

The Church is many important things. It is the kingdom of God on earth. It is the organization originally established by the Savior when he was here but lost from among men by apostasy. Doctrines and ordinances were changed, officers and offices abandoned and new ones initiated, spiritual gifts and authority lost, methods of worship totally altered. In our dispensation it has been restored by revelation from God through prophets, with the same organization, doctrines, ordinances, gifts of the Spirit, and authority it had in the days of Christ.

The Church is The Church of Jesus Christ of Latter-day Saints, restored to the earth with his divine gospel, for the blessing of all the children of God.

101

"I've Been Planning a Mission, but..."

"Bob, just today one of our neighbors told me about a young man your age who has brought six persons into the Church since he arrived in Vietnam several months ago. What do you think about that as a missionary experience and harvest?"

A few minutes later the three of them left the room, and the bishop stood by the door smiling gratefully. He thought of the response he'd seen in Bob's eyes as the nineteen-year-old's imagination had been caught by the question. The smile was one of affection and sympathetic understanding. The bishop, too, had been called from school and work and the security of home and loved ones to fulfill a military assignment in wartime. He could remember his own feelings, and he could imagine the anxieties the mom and dad were experiencing. For many, missions and all the other normal activities were now in jeopardy. The national emergency was again causing limitations on the number of eligible young men who could represent the Church as missionaries and Bob and many others of his generation would be called into the service without that experience behind them.

Dad had been shy, almost apologetic for being in the bishop's office, yet anxious to have this choice, much-loved son receive the encouraging counsel the bishop could give him. Mother was tearfully apprehensive for her boy. Bob himself showed his disappointment, but he was plainly willing and ready to serve where he was needed.

He wanted to know all about the service and asked many questions. Could he find friends who had his same standards? Would he be near Church groups and be permitted to associate with them? Would he see combat? How should he prepare for what lay ahead?

"No one can say for sure what your circumstances will be, Bob," the bishop told him, "but there are some things you can do to get ready. I suppose the most important thing to start with is attitude."

The bishop referred to his own experiences in the armed forces as he testified to Bob of the importance of the great adventure he was undertaking. "Military service can be a depressing and destructive undertaking, Bob," he said, "but it needn't be, and for you it must not be. Many of us who had been on missions discovered that we were in a position to do far more effective work for the Lord than we had ever done in the mission field. It can be exactly the same for you, if you have the wisdom and maturity to understand the nature of your opportunity, and if you make up your mind that it will be a mission. You will very likely have the opportunity to fulfill formal missionary service in the future, and you will do wonderfully effective work then if you look upon this experience as your first mission and make it a successful one. You can if you will." 103

When Bob left the bishop's office, he went with a very different feeling from the one with which he'd arrived. He was going on a mission after all—a mission for God and country! It would be tough and demanding, but with the right attitude and effort, he could and would make it. Bob carried with him a folded paper with some words he had written as the bishop had explained how he could be a missionary. These were the words:

> Serve God and my country
> Use time effectively, wisely. Waste none
> Learn, read, memorize. Fill mind with good things.
> Make friends, share with them, teach them.
> Live the gospel. Be cheerful be patient be clean—
>   body, mind, tongue.
> Pray regularly, with faith.
> Trust God. Love Christ.
> Choose wholesome companions. There are always some.
> Be a wholesome companion.
> Gather with the saints whenever you can.
> Be a district or stake missionary.

He knew that he would be tested and tried, that he would face opposition, be forced to choose, be privileged to sacrifice to pay back some of the debt he owed for the blessings of the gospel and the great heritage of his home in a free land.

He carried from the bishop's office a copy of a letter written during World War II by a soldier who had met a Mormon boy in a hospital, and whose life was changed by the experience. It was not very grammatical, and the spelling was imperfect, but it brought a tear to his eye and a chill to his spine. He got the message! He was going on a mission!

The letter:

Dear Sirs:

I am writting this letter, in accordance with my will and desire, which was a result of a few hours in an Army hospital.

There I met a soldier who was a Mormon. I became interested in his religion. Through him, I received words that have lived. Since then I have read a Book of Mormon.

I would like to receive information as to where I may purchase other books on the Mormon religion, so I may find understanding and find wisdom.

I have a great desire burning within my heart to learn of the Mormon religion, even to partake of it.

This Mormon soldier had something far greater than any other man I have ever met.

Where is the nearest Mormon chapel to me?

Sincerely yours,

John

Trailing Clouds of Glory

TRAILING CLOUDS OF GLORY

Our birth is but a sleep and a forgetting:
The Soul that rises with us, our life's Star,
Hath had elsewhere its setting,
And cometh from afar:
Not in entire forgetfulness,
And not in utter nakedness,
But trailing clouds of glory do we come
From God, who is our home:

William Wordsworth, who wrote the above lines in "Ode on Intimations of Immortality," had an almost prophetic view of man's meaning. He understood that our experience on this earth is one stage of an eternal journey, not a trip complete in itself. Like the prophets, he knew that birth is not the beginning of a person, nor is death the end. We came here "trailing clouds of glory . . . from God, who is our home," retaining only the dimmest occasional recollection of this earlier period of our existence. When we leave here through the door called "death," we go on to continued experience and opportunity. Only the body is laid aside for a while, like a heavy coat we take off in the spring. We take it up again someday, in God's good time, in the resurrection, when the body and spirit recombine as an eternal soul and we can begin to experience the "fulness of joy" which our Heavenly Father wants us to have.

> *"And the spirit and the body are the soul of man."*
> (D&C 88:15.)

> *"For man is spirit. The elements are eternal, and*
> *spirit and element, inseparably connected, receive*
> *a fulness of joy."* (D&C 93:33.)

These truths have been plainly taught by the prophets of God, and some of the poets have seemed to perceive them, also. Have you recently carefully read Eliza R. Snow's beautiful words to the hymn "O My Father"?

> *O my Father, thou that dwellest*
> *In the high and glorious place!*
> *When shall I regain thy presence,*
> *And again behold thy face?*
> *In thy holy habitation,*
> *Did my spirit once reside;*
> *In my first primeval childhood,*
> *Was I nurtured near thy side?*

> *For a wise and glorious purpose*
> *Thou has placed me here on earth,*
> *And withheld the recollection*
> *Of my former friends and birth,*
> *Yet ofttimes a secret something*
> *Whispered, "You're a stranger here;"*
> *And I felt that I had wandered*
> *From a more exalted sphere.*

> *When I leave this frail existence,*
> *When I lay this mortal by,*
> *Father, Mother, may I meet you*
> *In your royal courts on high?*
> *Then at length, when I've completed*
> *All you sent me forth to do,*
> *With your mutual approbation*
> *Let me come and dwell with you.*

The major quest of man is to learn for himself what is the "wise and glorious purpose" for which he is placed on the earth. Another poet helps direct us:

"The whole purpose of the world seems to be to provide a physical basis for the growth of the spirit." (Goethe.)

Our most vital need and major mission is not the satisfaction of our physical wants and aspirations but the development of our spirit for the important creative work of eternal life, here and hereafter.

107

"Green Thoughts"

108

IT WAS A STRANGE TITLE for an editorial —certainly a different one: "Green Thoughts." My eyes wandered with mild curiosity past the heading to the first words, and the scattered rays of a casual involvement suddenly gathered into the beam of an intense concentration. I had never read words just like them before, and I had never personally visited in a city where they could with such validity be written. These were the first provocative sentences:

"It is a sad thing when people cease to dream of flowers, and dream only of vegetables. Such, however, is the plight of this city today. Let a hundred flowers bloom— we think only of potatoes, peas, and vegetable marrow."

The conclusion of the article was equally poignant:

"Pity that we have no time to look at the flowers. . . ."

It was a Calcutta, India, newspaper I was reading, purchased for a few Indian pennies on a street where, the night before, my companions and I had been sickened and sorrowed by sights and sounds of another world. People were starving, picking scraps from the gutter, begging and badgering, thousands of them sleeping in their rags in the streets. A hard-pressed government, earnestly struggling to survive the engulfing flood of hundreds of thousands of persons pouring into the city in ever-increasing waves, could not keep up with the problems.

For multitudes of young people in India, Africa, China, Korea, and elsewhere, the life an American teenager lives—even in the humblest circumstances—would be unbelievable. They couldn't comprehend the profusion of privileges and blessings most of you enjoy.

What green thoughts have you these days?
What green dreams?

If there are enough vegetables to keep away hunger, and a roof and a bed and an interested heart nearby, rejoice! Dream of flowers, and share part of their fragrance through a life of gratitude, of responsibility, and of genuine concern for others.

109

Why Be Obedient?

110   One of the glorious promises made by Christ to his people shortly before his crucifixion is recorded in John 14:21. This verse is particularly appropriate to the needs of our time and generation. Read again the promise:

> *"He that loveth me shall be loved of my Father, and I will love him, and will manifest myself to him."*

In the same verse, the Savior explained how we may show our love for him: *"He that hath my commandments, and keepeth them, he it is that loveth me."* He also said, *"If ye love me, keep my commandments."* (John 14:15.)

There are some appropriate questions young people sometimes ask about God's commandments and their responsibility to obey them. Consider these:

What Are the Commandments of God?

The Ten Commandments of Sinai are familiar to all of us. Read them again (and often) in Exodus chapter 20 or Deuteronomy chapter 5. Jesus repeated them in summary for the rich young man (Matthew 19:16-21), and answered the lawyer's challenging questions as to the "great commandment" with his masterful declaration:

"Thou shalt love the Lord thy God with all thy heart, and with all thy soul, and with all thy mind.

"This is the first and great commandment.

"And the second is like unto it, Thou shalt love thy neighbour as thyself.

"On these two commandments hang all the law and the prophets." (See Matthew 22:35-40.)

Other wonderful restatements of the commandments are found in the Book of Mormon (Mosiah 13:12-24) and the Doctrine and Covenants (59:5-13).

We are commanded to obey the "first principles" of the gospel (D&C 33:10-14), to live wholesomely and righteously, to endure with steadfastness in Christ, having " . . . hope, and a love of God and of all men" (2 Nephi 31:17-21), to pay our tithes and offerings, to give and serve and share. To "have" God's commandments, we must learn and understand them. This is our sacred responsibility.

Are Not God's Laws Too Restrictive, Too Negative?

God's commandments do set some plain boundaries. But they are more than limitations—they are meant to be lamps unto our feet. They light the paths where we should walk to true happiness and eternal salvation. All of us need direction and instruction, and occasional reproof:

"For the commandment is a lamp; and the law is light; and reproofs of instruction are the way of life." (Proverbs 6:23.)

The apostle Paul finished a summary of the commandments with a wonderful, affirmative challenge:

". . . and if there be any other commandment, it is briefly comprehended in this saying, namely, Thou shalt love thy neighbour as thyself." (Romans 13:9.)

What If We Ignore or Disobey the Commandments?

In one notable example, it is written that the sinner "lacketh understanding: he that doeth it destroyeth his own soul. A wound and dishonour shall he get; and his reproach shall not be wiped away." (Proverbs 6:32-33.)

The Book of Mormon teaches us that *"wickedness never was happiness"* (Alma 41:10) and that he that *"doeth iniquity, doeth it unto himself."* (Helaman 14:30.)

Sorrowfully, the blessing we might have had is lost to us if we sin and do not repent, and even the gracious pardon of our Lord to the repentant sinner will not recapture wasted opportunities for service and sharing and learning.

What Is the Result of Obedience to God's Commandments?

Christ's promise is that we may be assured of his love and the love of our Father, and that he will manifest himself to us. There can never be anything more important than this. Perhaps no one has better described the effects of obedience than did Paul when he wrote to his young friend and brother Timothy:

> "Now the end of the commandment is charity out of a pure heart, and of a good conscience, and of faith unfeigned." (1 Timothy 1:5.)

Consider these promises carefully:

A Good Conscience: To feel right with oneself.

Charity out of a Pure Heart: To be genuinely concerned for others . . . to care, to serve, to give, to love. Good conscience leads to such unselfish interest in others, and to

Faith Unfeigned: To truly trust in God and in the fulfilment of his purposes for us.

For this mortal life and its complexities, there are no more significant blessings than these, none to be more desired. And all of them have eternal implications, the quality of carry-over. Add to them one other of the sweetest promises of the Lord, and the case for obedience is wonderfully clear:

> " . . . *let virtue garnish thy thoughts unceasingly; then shall thy confidence wax strong in the presence of God; and . . . . the Holy Ghost shall be thy constant companion . . . .*

—D&C 121:45-46

A Heritage You Earn

*"What from your fathers'
heritage is lent, earn it
anew to really possess it."*

—Goethe

The lovely girl who was speaking was a high school student from a small town. She was in Washington as a delegate to a conference of youth and youth leaders from across the globe, and she was thrilled and excited at the things she had seen and heard and experienced in her country's capital.

The audience was a difficult one for so young and inexperienced a speaker, but the Senators and Congressmen and other leaders present gave her rapt attention. All eyes and ears—and minds and hearts, too—were hers as she delivered her message. There was something about the urgency and intensity and genuineness of it that caught up everyone there. She had stood before the Lincoln Memorial and the Washington Monument, had learned to know other people from many lands, had been away for a time from her loved ones, had thought and learned and prayed. She had something to share.

"It has been a great privilege for me to be here for these few days," she said, "and I will never forget the experience. Before I came I thought I loved my family. I thought I loved my country. I thought I loved my Church. But oh I just didn't know! I just didn't know!" She helped many others of us to know, that day, far better than we had ever known before, how much we, too, loved our families, our countries, and our Church.

What about you?—in Bristol or Montevideo or Orleans or Atlanta or Veracruz, or wherever you may be among the multitudes of places the world over—have you begun to "earn" and "really possess" the great blessings of your choice historical and spiritual heritage by learning of them and appreciating them and living in such a way that you can help to preserve and increase them for those who follow after you? They are worth everything. Your children and their children have a right to enjoy them, also.

114

Transmit a Miracle

It is said the greatest of all miracles was the change that occurred in the lives of those who were touched by Jesus. Think of Peter, and Paul, and Magdalene, and others—many—since. . . . Is it an extension of that miracle?—or a greater miracle still?—that those who have been transformed by the Master's hand can themselves transmit the marvelous gift to others? . . . There are wonderful thoughts to think at Christmas, important feelings to experience, choice gifts to give in the name of Christ.

The beggar could be pitied, and permitted his pitiful begging. He had never walked; he had been lame all his life. Every day he was carried to the temple gate where he could plead for alms from those who entered the sacred building. . . . One day, soon after the death and resurrection of Jesus and the glorious manifestation of the Spirit at Pentecost, Peter and John passed by the cripple on their way into the temple. He asked them for money. Peter looked at him with compassion and love, and the man, seeing this, expected a generous gift. Peter said to him, "Look on us." . . . Then, "Silver and gold have I none; but such as I have give I thee: In the name of Jesus Christ of Nazareth, rise up and walk." . . . "And he took him by the right hand, and lifted him up." . . . "And he, leaping up stood, and walked, and entered with them into the temple, walking, and leaping, and praising God."

There are gifts we can give, through Jesus, and by the power he has given us, marvelous gifts of spiritual strength and sympathy and love. And not the least of these is to stretch forth our hand to our brother and lift him up.

"Be Ye Separate"

*" . . . all you that are desirous to follow the voice
of the good shepherd, come ye out from the wicked, and
be ye separate, and touch not their unclean things; . . . "*
—Alma 5:57

" . . . be ye clean, that bear the vessels of the Lord."
—Isaiah 52:11

The two handsome young deacons reverently passing the sacrament of the Lord's Supper to the small British congregation reminded one of other fine Latter-day Saint young men performing similar service for the Master all over the globe. They were twelve years old, clean, wholesome, manly, clear-eyed boys. Quietly and worshipfully they completed their sacred assignment and took their chairs in the congregation with the other members of the Church. I sat watching gratefully, thinking of the Good Shepherd and repeating to myself the words . . .

" . . . be ye separate. . . . "

" . . . be ye clean, that bear the vessels of the Lord."

116

A Distinction with a Difference

It is truly a *distinction* to be a member of The Church of Jesus Christ of Latter-day Saints, if being one makes you *different* from what you otherwise might be and from what the crowd often is. Young people often dislike the notion of being *different*, they like to be one of the gang. Your parents and teachers and Church leaders know this and understand the need for youth to be accepted and respected. But they also know that a Mormon boy or girl must sometimes choose between being "accepted" by the wrong crowd or "respected" by the right one. They know that the Lord has spoken plainly on the subject, saying:

> *"Come ye out from the wicked"*
> *"Be ye separate"*
> *"Touch not their unclean things"*

Does this need much interpretation or application to your particular circumstances?

Think now about your immediate future. Young men, think of bearing the sacrament trays, of breaking the bread and preparing the water, of kneeling to utter the sacred blessing. Think of holding your missionary credentials. Think of placing your hands on the head of a person who is ill to bless him, or of taking the hand of your bride in the holy temple, or of holding your own infant in your arms and to give it a name and blessing before a congregation of the Saints.

Lovely girls, think of accepting the hand of your chosen one in the temple, consider the caress of your fingertips on your baby's lips, your cool hand on a loved one's fevered brow.

117

"BE YE SEPARATE . . . " "BE YE CLEAN, THAT BEAR THE
VESSELS OF THE LORD . . . "

Something More Than Bravery

IT IS GOOD TO BE BRAVE IN THE FACE OF DANGER OR DISASTER OR DEATH.

But to endure in the face of adversity . . . to discipline resolutely the drives of desire and appetite . . . to establish worthy goals and strive for them . . . to choose noble ideals and live by them . . . to serve worthy causes selflessly, sacrificially . . . to meet stalwartly the relentless commonplace challenges of the eternal everyday,

THIS DEMANDS SOMETHING MORE THAN BRAVERY . . . IT DEMANDS MORAL COURAGE AND A LOFTY SENSE OF RESPONSIBILITY AND RELATIONSHIP TO GOD AND MAN.

Physical fearlessness may be forced and temporary. It may have an unworthy motivation or expression. Thieves and bullies and cutthroats have a certain degree of bravery.

True moral courage expresses itself in character and discipline, in moral living, in participating citizenship, in an earnest search for truth, in preserving faith and conviction and honor, in avoiding dishonor and conduct that leads to self-contempt.

On several occasions J. Edgar Hoover has written on the subject of moral courage and moral living, using as his model Sam Cowley, "the highest example of good it has been my pleasure to know."

Samuel Parkinson Cowley was the son of an apostle and brother of another.

He served as a missionary in Hawaii and remained an active, devoted member of the Church. Elder Cowley joined the Federal Bureau of Investigation in its infancy, earned the high rank of inspector, and gained enduring glory for his heroism in ending the careers of two depraved murderers, John Dillinger and "Baby Face" Nelson. He died after a gun battle in which Nelson was killed.

At his funeral a friend said of Brother Cowley: "I have thought that his name should have been Peter. He was a veritable rock to those who knew, who loved and trusted him. His was the calm of a man who did his best and left the final decision to a Higher Power."

Mr. Hoover has paid Sam Cowley his highest tribute of respect for heroism, for bravery which included but transcended physical courage. He said of Samuel Cowley's death: "This sacrifice was not just a magnificent demonstration of momentary heroism. It was the culmination of that greatest of all adventures in moral courage—a truly moral life."

Bravery, with proper purpose and motivation, may lead to heroic action; without proper goals and discipline it can be dangerous and destructive.

Moral courage is steady,. being the foundation of devotion to duty, loyalty, and trust. It expresses itself through
strong minds,
great hearts,
ready hands,
true faith.

Moral courage is SOMETHING MORE THAN BRAVERY.

"Be strong and of good courage; be not afraid, neither be thou dismayed: for the Lord thy God is with thee whithersoever thou goest."
—Joshua 1:9

Take a Giant Step

"To every thing there is a season, and a time to every purpose under the heaven."
—Ecclesiastes 3:1

120

THE SEASON IS SUMMER—usually a quieter and probably less pressured time, and a good time to work and rest and play and to get better acquainted with the family.

How would you like this to be the very best summer ever?

Could this be the season when you take that exciting giant step toward a knowledge—*for yourself*—of scripture, the word of the Lord?

It will take some reading and thinking and some discussion with one or more special people who like to stretch a bit and who care about learning worthwhile things. But you'll love it, if you're ready.

A Place to Start

About twenty-seven hundred years ago a group of people who seemed sincere were fasting and praying and "afflicting" themselves with sackcloth and ashes, believing they were pleasing the Lord. He told them he didn't like what they were doing and gave them some directions about what they should do to be happy and to live constructively and thus to please him.

For Us, Too

In these instructions the Lord asks something of us and our generation. What is he asking us to do? What does he say the results will be? Think about it and talk it over and mark it in your Bible. Then "LET IT WORK IN YOU!"

Loose the bands of wickedness . . .
Undo the heavy burdens . . .
Let the oppressed go free . . .
Break every yoke . . .
Deal thy bread to the hungry . . .
Bring into thy house the poor that are cast out . . .
Cover the naked . . .
Hide not thyself from thine own flesh . . .
Take away from the midst of thee the yoke,
*   the putting forth of the finger, and speaking vanity . . .*
Draw out thy soul to the hungry . . .
Satisfy the afflicted soul . . .
Honor the Lord in the way you keep the Sabbath.
                    —See Isaiah 58:6-10, 13

121

You can build a summer's fun *(and a worthwhile life)* on learning to understand and carry out these directions from God. Some are easy to understand. Some require real thought. Think what they mean to you and how they can apply to your life and circumstances.

Formula for Success

122   Suppose you've been called to be Sunday School secretary, or an assistant Scoutmaster, or a member of the youth committee. Would you like to succeed?

One who has an assignment in the Church, and studies and prays but does not work, is not happy and not successful. One who really works with all his heart, might, mind, and strength will soon know his need for study and prayer and will seek them.

Over the years most of us have heard the basic formula of missionary success: *study, work, pray.* The same principles are fundamental in any other service opportunity for the Lord or his children. And *work* is certainly not the least among them.

Work is the key to full joy in the plan of the Lord. A young person who learns to work is laying for himself a foundation upon which all future achievement can rise. He will never lack for opportunity and sweet experience in the years ahead.

How Shall We Work?

Anxiously:	Of our own free will.
Cheerfully:	"Let cheerfulness abound with industry."
Diligently:	"There is no excellence without labor."
Honestly:	"Thou shalt not idle away thy time."

Effectively:	"What e'er thou art, act well thy part."
Courageously:	"Be not afraid of their faces. . . . "
Persistently:	Steadiness and consistency and resoluteness win!
Patiently:	"Learn to labor and to wait." He who works while he endures will prevail.
With the long view:	Work where you are, "as for years."
Faithfully:	Be true to trust. It is a tribute to be trusted.
With the Spirit:	No labor for the Lord can succeed without his Spirit.

Why?

Because the Lord has commanded it. Because you agreed to. Because you want to. Because it is right.

Where?

Where you are, in your present assignment. "Happy Valley" is not someplace else, doing something else. "Cast down your bucket where you are."

123

When?

Now? Today! The field is white, all ready to harvest! There are few virtues so holy or glorious or important as *work*.

Through the Valley

124

It was six o'clock on a beautiful midsummer Sabbath morning in Philadelphia, and I was on my way to Valley Forge to speak to a group of Boy Scouts. There were no other cars on the streets, and the driver seemed a bit annoyed to have to stop at a red traffic signal at the intersection. But I was glad. On a vacant lot on the corner I saw a historical marker carrying this message:

> *This is the site of the home*
> *where Thomas Jefferson wrote*
> *the Declaration of Independence*
> *1776*

All the way to Valley Forge I thought about that marker and about the marvelous declaration of conviction and commitment that had come from that unostentatious place. The Declaration of Independence was a great statement of principle. "This is what we believe," it said, "and this is where we stand. In defense of these principles we commit our lives, our fortunes, and our sacred honor."

As I stood to speak to the Scouts, I saw, looming over the trees, the top of the great arch dedicated to the heroes of the revolution. The names of George Washington and General Anthony Wayne were there, and many others, but my gaze was fixed on the dates at the end of the writing: 1777-78.

In 1776 the Colonials made their declaration of principle. Not many months later, in the very valley where the Boy Scouts now visited, they had their chance to prove they meant it. It was so cold in that valley that winter that many men froze to death. There were so few provisions that many men starved to death. Of the eleven thousand who started the winter, only eight thousand survived. Their three thousand comrades were buried there in unmistakable witness of the sincerity of their faith in the cause.

Life has its great times of commitment, and the valleys that inevitably follow. A convert covenants and almost certainly walks thereafter through his valley of trial. Two wonderful young people kneel at an altar and covenant with each other and God, and then move into their adventure and learn that marriage requires a courageous walk through valleys that are sometimes difficult.

So with every major experience of life. There is the commitment and the opportunity to meet the subsequent tests. There is the declaration and the valley, and there is the inevitable triumph when courage and quality meet the tests.

Live
and
Learn

The Lord has sternly warned against the egotism and arrogance, the foolish pride and rebelliousness that sometimes accompany learning. Acquiring and applying knowledge with intelligence —"the light of truth"—and with humility, is indispensable to our happiness and exaltation.

" . . . O the vainness, and the frailties, and the foolishness of men! When they are learned they think they are wise, and they hearken not unto the counsel of God, for they set it aside, supposing they know of themselves, wherefore, their wisdom is foolishness and it profiteth them not. And they shall perish.

"But to be learned is good if they hearken unto the counsels of God." (2 Nephi 9:28, 29.)

Among the unique values which have brought The Church of Jesus Christ of Latter-day Saints most favorable attention from interested observers is its attitude toward learning. Utah, center of Mormonism, ranks at the top of American states in educational effort and results, and in the production of leading men of science and of achievement. Other areas with large LDS membership have had similar results.

What are the reasons for this record?

To members of the Church, acquiring knowledge and growing in intelligence are principles of religious faith and action. Consider what the scriptures teach about these principles:

Learning Is Commanded by God and Is Pleasing to Him.

" . . . study and learn, . . . " (D&C 90:15.)

" . . . seek ye out of the best books words of wisdom; seek learning, . . . " (D&C 88:118.)

"The glory of God is intelligence, . . . " (D&C 93:36.)

Knowledge and Intelligence Are Essential to Salvation.

"It is impossible for a man to be saved in ignorance." (D&C 131:6.)

"Whatever principle of intelligence we attain unto in this life, it will rise with us in the resurrection.

"And if a person gains more knowledge and intelligence . . . than another, he will have so much the advantage in the world to come." (D&C 130:18-19.)

" . . . it is my will that you should . . . obtain a knowledge of history, and of countries, and of kingdoms, of laws of God and man, and all this for the salvation of Zion." (D&C 93:53.)

Learning Should Be Broad and Deep, Including "All Things . . . That Pertain unto the Kingdom of God."

"And I give unto you a commandment that you shall teach one another the doctrine of the kingdom.

" . . . that you may be instructed more perfectly in theory, in principle, in doctrine, in the law of the gospel, in all things that pertain unto the kingdom of God, that are expedient for you to understand;

"Of things both in heaven and in the earth, and under the earth; things which have been, . . . which are, . . . which must shortly come to pass; things which are at home . . . which are abroad; the wars and the perplexities of the nations, and the judgments which are on the land; and a knowledge also of countries and of kingdoms—" (D&C 88:77-78.)

" . . . become acquainted with all good books, and with languages, tongues, and people." (D&C 90:15.)

" . . . obtain a knowledge of history, and . . . of laws of God and man, . . . " (D&C 93:53.)

Wide Learning Is a Qualification for Service to the Lord.

"That ye may be prepared in all things when I shall send you again to magnify the calling whereunto I have called you, and the mission with which I have commissioned you.

"Behold, I sent you out to testify and warn the people, and it becometh every man who hath been warned to warn his neighbor." (D&C 88:80-81.)

Learning May Be Gained Through Search, Study, Diligence, Obedience, and Through Faith and Prayer.

" . . . seek ye diligently . . . seek learning, even by study and also by faith." (D&C 88:118.)

" . . . if a person gains more knowledge and intelligence in this life through his diligence and obedience . . . he will have so much the advantage. . . . " (D&C 130:19.)

It Must Demonstrate Its Value in Right-Thinking and Well-Doing, in Motivating Obedience to the Commandments of God.

" . . . to be learned is good if they hearken unto the counsels of God." (2 Nephi 9:29.)

" . . . let every man learn his duty, and to act in the office in which he is appointed, in all diligence." (D&C 107:99.)

" . . . if ye believe all these things, see that ye do them." (Mosiah 4:10.)

Learning Imposes an Obligation to Share and Serve.

" . . . teach one another according to the office wherewith I have appointed you; . . . words of wisdom, . . . the doctrine of the kingdom." (D&C 38:23, 88:118; 88:77.)

Toward Quality Decisions

More things in life are certain than the oft-noted "death and taxes." One of the certainties of life is that individuals must make decisions. Another is that the quality of our decisions determines the success, satisfaction, and contribution of our lives.

But how does one go about making right decisions? How to avoid the wrong choices, and the "decisions by default" which are the product of indecision?

Here are some suggestions for consideration:

BE CLEAR ON YOUR PRINCIPLES. Decisions involving honor, honesty, virtue decide themselves, if we have learned what is right and firmly committed ourselves to it beforehand. Deciding on the basis of correct principles habituates us to right choices and strengthens our capacity to discern and choose the good.

But what of decisions which are not so clear, where there may be "right" in both or several alternatives?

TAKE THE LONG VIEW, LOOK AHEAD. What do you

really want to give and get from life?

Some of us make shortsighted choices which seem to serve the needs or desires of the moment. How will the decision look in an hour, a month, five years, eternally? What effect will it have on you then?

THINK AND CONSIDER, EXAMINE AND WEIGH. Learn all you can about the issues, then evaluate. Perhaps it would be well to write down on paper the "fors" and "againsts" of a particular solution, clarifying the issues and prospects.

No important decisions should be made in haste when time for deliberation is possible, and none should be made in anger or sorrow or anxiety.

LEARN FROM THE EXPERIENCE OF OTHERS. Look around you. Listen. Be wise enough not to make the mistakes others have made. Jesus was able to learn without the painful problems of wrong choices. He accepted the counsel and direction of his Father and the prophets. This should be our objective and pattern.

COUNSEL WITH WISE AND EXPERIENCED FRIENDS. We cannot shift the burden of making decisions. We must become self-reliant. But there are those who can help us clarify our objectives and thinking. God has commissioned some to counsel, and promised them discernment in so doing.

Advice from the unqualified, whose own choices are often obviously bad, must be avoided or resisted.

PRAY. Seek the help of the Lord in considering, in deciding. The guidance of the Spirit is promised those who humble themselves and qualify.

DECIDE, AND PRAY. On the basis of principle, with the long view, having thought and observed and counseled, prayerfully make the decision. The Lord will not decide for us, but he will give us confirming witness if we have chosen well.

Recall the experience of Oliver Cowdery who tried to translate but failed. To him the Lord said: "Behold you have not understood; you have supposed that I would give it unto you, when you took no thought save it was to ask me. But, behold, I say unto you, that you must study it out in your mind; then you must ask me if it be right, and if it is right I will cause that your bosom shall burn within you; therefore, you shall feel that it is right." (D&C 9:7-9.)

130

How
to Be
Constant
Amidst
Change

Change is
a key word often
used to describe our
times and the great
challenges facing your generation. What kind of changes?
Job opportunities . . . are increasing in
number and kind. National Health Council is
able to identify more than 150 careers in the
field of health. A recent manual listed approximately fifty
newly minted names of scientific specializations unheard of
a few years ago, ranging from astrobiodynamics to zymo-
crystallography.

Population . . . increasing in number and mobility.

Nearly 20 percent of the civilian population yearly change
their place of residence in the United States. This is similarly
true in other countries.

Cities reach out like the octopus and swallow up what once was "country" area. Suburbia expands and rolls on.

Transportation and communication . . . the world is shrinking.

Fantastic advances in these fields bring even the feats of conquering the universe into our front room.

Experience and relationships often undreamed of in times past are now yours.

The many facets of entertainment and learning are startling when compared with possibilities of years past.

Yet with all of the change and the increasing number of choices to be made, one wonderful fact deserves special attention: Young members of The Church of Jesus Christ of Latter-day Saints who choose to learn and live and serve and share the gospel continue to grow wonderfully, to participate and contribute, to excel in important ways, to have sweet associations and wholesome companionships, to enjoy firm friendships and sensible courtship, to marry and live happily, to find joy!

Kenya, England, America

A recent London Stake conference offered a compelling example. Several young speakers took part, one of them a lovely young woman from Kenya who joined the Church a few months before while attending college in London. Talented musically and in many other ways, she has been very active in the Church. At Christmas she returned to Kenya to explain her important decision to her beloved bother. Back in London, she had lunch, on the day of her baptism, with her uncle, a minister in another church. When he had talked with Judy, this honorable man advised her to go ahead and be baptized, saying that he could see and sense in her that she had found what she wanted and was happy. Still the only member of her family in the Church, she has and exudes the happiness and goodness the gospel brings.

Another speaker was an American girl, member of a building program missionary family living in Epsom, England. She has become a recognized leader among her associates, and is a great missionary for the Lord. Her talk, like Judy's, was thrilling and inspiring, and so were those delivered by the wonderful British boy and girl who followed. Each was a strong example of the effectiveness of Church principles and programs applied in the lives of youth. In the congregation were many others who could have done as well, and so are there among Church youth all over the world.

Troubles, Too Many

There are troubles among the young, true, too frequent and often tragic troubles. Always they come through failure on someone's part to understand and live the principles of the gospel of Jesus Christ. Unfavorable home circumstances, poor adult example, unwise companionships, temptations imposed by people who sell evil for money, wrong choices—all of these contribute to sin and sorrow among the young. All could be avoided through the application of the principles of the gospel.

The marvelous thing is the steadiness and faithfulness of so many wonderful young people. We love the constant examples we find among you of initiative, self-reliance, responsibility, thrift and frugality, thoughtfulness, service and generosity.

We are grateful for your honesty and integrity, your desire to know the truth; for your sensitivity to beauty and idealism, your respect for the viewpoints of others.

We love your loyalty, your love for country and for truth, your willingness to serve and give; the courage you have to stand steady in the right.

133

We thank God for your faith, your fortitude, your future.

We know our Heavenly Father will help you to choose well, to accept changes wisely, to get right with him and your fellowmen, to do good and feel good. God bless you to be constant amid the change!

Happiness
and
Honor

134

If one finds real happiness, he must have an enduring and satisfying appreciation for his national heritage. All over America and in certain countries elsewhere youth are being taught the great truth that what they do matters to their country, that to strengthen character is to strengthen the nation.

The United States Air Force Academy has a motto: "We will not lie, cheat, or steal, or tolerate among us one who does." Now, you figure out what that means in terms of *you*. You figure out what that means in terms of personal responsibility and responsibility other than for oneself. What it means is that what you do in that automobile, what you do in that classroom, or business place, or lunch line matters. If anything stands out clearly now to people who are apprehensive about impending international incineration, it is that what we are, individually, matters—infinitely much. It matters to our country; it matters to our happiness.

Theodore Roosevelt said these words:

"I preach to you, my countrymen, that our country calls not for a life of ease, but for a life of strenuous endeavor. If we stand idly by, if we seek merely slow and slothful ease and ignoble peace, if we shrink from the hard contests where men must win at hazard of their lives and at the risk of all they hold dear, then the bolder and stronger peoples will pass us by and will win for themselves the domination of the world."

This speaks not alone of our ability to stand up to the Communists and say, "You drop the bomb, and we drop one." It talks of what is inside the individual American citizen—how much he cares, what he is willing to give.

I listened to President Harold B. Lee interview men for important Church responsibilities one day, and one of the things he asked some of them was, "What are you willing to give, to sacrifice?" The answers were interesting.

Now I ask you, what are you willing to give for your country? Your life? Most of you would admit to this. But are you willing to LIVE now, that the spiritual and moral core of this nation may have the benefit of your strength?

It matters, and it matters to your happiness.

The Keys of Harmony

Have you watched an accomplished violinist who is about to perform at a symphony or other concert or at a church meeting? Even though he has tuned his instrument previously, if he is a good violinist, he will at the last moment touch the bow to the strings again, making sure the violin is in tune.

Have you wondered why a musician would do this? Occasionally someone is critical, even wondering aloud "why he didn't tune it before he came." He did! But a violin is such a sensitive instrument that any slight change of circumstances—a bump, the touch of a warm hand, a change of temperature—can alter the delicate balance of its attunement and turn *consonance* into *dissonance*. A pleasing and harmonious balance of tones can become an unpleasant and unlovely *dis*harmony, just through some small incident or disturbance.

Human beings are like violins. We too are sensitive and responsive to conditions around us. A cheerful and happy balance can be upset by a small incident or unpleasant occurrence. Harmony can turn into discord through a small "bump" or a "change in temperature."

Violins are tuned by turning a key which slightly alters the tension on the violin string and thus changes the pitch.

People have a way of getting in tune, also. We can do this through prayer and search and meditation. Even if we have "tuned up" a little while before, it is good to remember that we need to *stay* in tune, and that we must check up on this regularly. Especially is this true when we are going to do something which is of service to God and our fellowmen. This is why Nephi told his beloved brethren that they *"must pray always, and not faint; that ye must not perform any thing unto the Lord save in the first place ye shall pray unto the Father in the name of Christ, that he will consecrate thy performance. . . . "* (2 Nephi 32:9.)

137

Tune up, and stay in tune, always.

Doing What Has to Be Done

Sometimes we think of courage as the opposite of fear. But courage is something more, as many of us had re-emphasized for us one night in a small room in "The Brinks" in mid-Saigon.

The young captain who spoke had his head bowed in humility and emotion as he took his turn in the circle of men who were testifying to each other. He had arrived in Vietnam as the pilot of a huge bomber but had been assigned immediately as a forward air controller. The small single-engine planes he and his companions flew were extremely vulnerable to enemy fire, and the job they were assigned was a highly dangerous one.

"Every time I approach the airplane I am tempted to run away," he said. "And every time I take off I feel like flying so high the enemy can't hit me. Of course, I do take off and I fly low where I can do my job, over the jungles and the canals and the rice paddies. When I see something unusual, or when I draw enemy fire, I call in the artillery or the air strikes and stay around spotting and doing my job. While I fly, I sing the songs of Zion and talk to God and think of my wife and wonderful children at home."

The captain told of an incident over a troubled area where he had stayed to spot for the artillery, only to find himself encompassed by encroaching darkness when he finally headed home. He had no navigational instruments, and there was neither a sight nor a sound that could guide him. He was totally lost and unable to find his way home. Praying and thinking of his family, he flew low, knowing the possibility of destruction through collision with a tree or hill or barrier but desperately seeking a place to land. Through the darkness and the clouds he spotted what appeared to be a flat place, and he safely landed his plane on it.

As he waited out the night, not knowing where he was or what moment trouble might arrive, he prayed and sang and thought again of his loved ones. When dawn came, he found himself on the half-usable airstrip of an abandoned rubber plantation, and he took off and returned home without incident.

As he talked, I knew all over again that courage is not the absence of fear; true courage is manifested in bravely doing what has to be done in spite of fears or foes or the foolishness of the crowd or the taunts of the group. True courage is doing the right thing in spite of the odds or opposition or apprehension.

139

What's Missing? U-R!

140 The slogans on the bulletin board of the Lutheran Church youth room were attention-getters and thought-provokers. The two Latter-day Saint missionaries and other young Mormon visitors stopped to read them:

> CH - - CH
> *What's Missing!*
> U - R!

The visit was a choice experience! The Lutheran young people were gracious hosts. They listened intently and respectfully to the missionary presentation, asked thoughtful questions, and accepted the proffered literature warmly. The members of the MIA group who made the visit were impressed with their friendliness and their obviously genuine religious commitment.

Principles of faith and personal conviction were discussed in a spirit of sympathy and honest inquiry. The two groups found common ground in Christ, as well as some differing viewpoints, and further discussions were arranged with anticipation.

How important it is, as we grow in the strength of our convictions through search and service and reverence, that we appreciate the value and virtue in others and that we learn to walk arm in arm with them toward common objectives!

On the day the gospel was first preached in England, the Lord gave through Joseph Smith to one of his associates this important admonition of love and fellowship:

"I know thy heart, and have heard thy prayers concerning thy brethren. Be not partial towards them in love above many others, but let thy love be for them as for thyself; and let thy love abound unto all men, and unto all who love my name."

—D&C 112:11

To this the Prophet added a strong statement of great meaning:

" . . . we ought to be aware of those prejudices which sometimes so strangely present themselves, and are so congenial to human nature, against our friends, neighbors, and brethren of the world, who choose to differ from us in opinion and in matters of faith. Our religion is between us and our God. Their religion is between them and their God.

"There is a love from God that should be exercised toward those of our faith, who walk uprightly, which is peculiar to itself, but it is without prejudice; it gives scope to the mind, which enables us to conduct ourselves with greater liberality towards all that are not of our faith, than what they exercise toward one another."

—*Teachings of the Prophet Joseph Smith, pp. 146-147.*

141

We do not compromise our convictions and devotion when we recognize the worth of others as individuals and work earnestly with those who share our desire to achieve wholesome objectives. True to our faith, fearless in defense of it, exemplary in its application, we manifest our mature understanding of it by conducting ourselves *"with greater liberality towards all that are not of our faith, than what they exercise toward one another."*

Every Man in
His Own Place

The Rotary Club president had a puzzled look on his face as he repeated his question to the rugged, intense high school boy seated across from him: *"Why can't you go with the others? If it is a matter of finances we can handle it. If it's a problem to get away from your job at the drugstore, I am sure we can work this out with your employer. What is the problem?"*

The young man looked the president calmly in the eye and said, "I'm sorry, sir. I do appreciate the chance to get in on this wonderful experience. I appreciate the generosity of the Rotary Club in sponsoring this trip and the conference, and I wish I could go. The reason I can't is that I am superintendent of the Sunday School in my church. I have been encouraging the other teachers and officers to be regular and faithful in their attendance, and I just can't take two weeks off from my assignment. It wouldn't be right."

142

The club president said goodbye to the young man with a sense of wonderment. He and other outstanding high school athletes who were scholastically strong and active in school leadership had been invited to enjoy a vacation workshop under the direction of leading men in the large city. Every other young person invited had responded eagerly. This Mormon boy was different. The man marveled that a seventeen-year-old boy could be so interested in fulfilling a responsibility.

All over the Church there are choice young people like this, committed enough and mature enough to serve unselfishly in various responsibilities in the Church. In some areas where there are fewer members of the Church young people carry a heavier burden—and they do it well.

Whether the assignment given us is highly significant or seemingly insignificant, our service is important. President McKay has said: *"Much of the progress of the Church is due to the application of a fundamental principle of soul growth . . . individual responsibility."*

President McKay was speaking consistently with the statement of the Prophet Joseph Smith, who said: *"Let the Saints remember that great things depend on their individual exertion, and that they are called to be co-workers with us and the Holy Spirit in accomplishing the great work of the last days. . . . "*

To accept an assignment in the right spirit, to learn the job and to do it, to develop dependability and unselfishness and sincere concern for others—these are within the capability of the young people of this generation. The Lord alone knows our hearts, but all of those around us get a clear concept of our sincerity through the manner in which we accept and fulfill opportunities for service.

143

Brother Larry Powell, a former Baptist minister who joined the Church during World War II and was faithful in every calling, wrote these wonderful words:

> *"If Joseph Smith, one man committed to God, can do what has been done in the brief time that has elapsed, think what could be accomplished by a similar dedication and consecration by the hundreds of thousands of priests today! Is it too much to ask? Isn't it within the realm of possibility?*
>
> *"I who am the least of all elders, less than two years old as holder of the office, feel that the bringing in of the kingdom of our God and his Son is just as much my responsibility in my office as it is David O. McKay's in his. We bear the same priesthood, with its responsibilities. True, some have certain keys and callings that an elder doesn't have, but the effectiveness with which they fill the responsibilities of their office depends in no small measure upon our faithfulness in our offices. 'They all stood round about the camp, every man in HIS OWN PLACE.' The battle was won."*

Greater Love Hath No Man

144

When Jim Childers turned twelve, he received a choice letter from his big brother, Steve, who was a cadet at West Point. That letter meant a great deal to Jim, especially later.

Dear Jim: Happy Birthday! How does it feel to be twelve? If I
were home, it would feel painful in a certain spot . . . understand?
By the time you get this you will be twelve. This is an important
time in your life because you will be able to hold the priesthood
now. I wish I could be there when you are ordained. You
must always remember that holding the priesthood is a great honor
and privilege. You must always be true to it even if you see
others who aren't honoring theirs. The office of deacon in the
Aaronic Priesthood gives you more power and authority in God's
kingdom than do the offices of President of the United States,
Prime Minister of Great Britain, and leaders of all the other countries
combined. It may be hard to realize, but it does. Don't
think the seriousness of the priesthood will make holding it
unpleasant, for you will find that the priesthood will give you
great opportunities for service. Love of God and service to him,

combined with love and service to people is the best road to
happiness. You have a wonderful opportunity unfolding before
you; make the most of it. Honor and magnify your priesthood.
If you are in doubt whether something is right or wrong, ask
yourself, "Would Jesus do it?" If he wouldn't, don't you,
and you won't be wrong. I hope you have a Happy Birthday.
Don't bother your sister too much. Write me and tell me
what you are doing.

Your brother, Steve

On January 19, 1967, two days before Jim's nineteenth
birthday, his brother Steve—Captain Stephen A. Childers, United
States Army—died heroically while attempting to save the lives
of women and children held as hostages by enemy troops in a cave
in the central highlands of South Vietnam.

Captain Childers, an infantry company commander, volunteered for duty in Vietnam after service in Europe. When some
of his men were wounded while seeking to evacuate the hostages,
Captain Childers himself went into the cave to try to free them
and was killed by enemy fire.

Steve Childers' departure from this world was entirely consistent with the way he lived in it during his short but brimful and
overflowing twenty-six years. His was a balanced and productive
life, marked by success and honor as a student, athlete, leader,
outstanding soldier, and by an unswerving devotion to God, to the
Church, and to his fellowmen. At West Point, from which he was
graduated in 1963, he was group leader of the Latter-day Saint
cadets. One closely connected with the Academy for many years
wrote this of Steve's activities at the Point:

145

> *"In the four years he was at West Point we came
> to know him well. We have never known one of 'our
> boys' who radiated so much good or inspired so much
> confidence as Steve. Every cadet, and especially every
> LDS cadet, whose spirit needed bolstering was a better,
> stronger person for having known Steve. His testimony
> and faith were contagious and all the more inspiring be-
> cause they came from a man who was an all-round per-
> son."*

Letter after letter received by Captain Childers' parents from
many parts of the world spoke of his unusual love for children and

of their great love for him, of his deep religious conviction, wholesome life, and selfless service.

Many choice LDS men have given their lives in the cause of freedom. It is well that young members of the Church, and all others who may read, soberly consider the noble sacrifice of Elder Stephen A. Childers, who gave his life in defense of freedom and in an effort to preserve the lives of innocent women and children. He serves as an appropriate example of the men who lay their lives on the altar that others may live in freedom and in peace.

"Greater love hath no man than this, that a man lay down his life for his friends." (John 15:13.)

146

Theological Illiterates

In a recent conversation with a choice college girl, I listened to two statements that may reflect the feelings of many of her peers who have similar problems for similar reasons and who, like her, seem content to understand where the solutions are without doing anything to bring them about.

She called herself a "theological illiterate," shortly thereafter noting that she has never read through any of the so-called standard works nor any basic exposition of gospel principles. She had not read any version of Church history, lengthy or abbreviated.

I recalled for her a statement made by Dr. John A. Widtsoe, learned apostle and university president, in his great autobiography, *In a Sunlit Land*. Dr. Widtsoe wrote:

"Since my boyhood I had known the restored gospel to be true. In my college days I had subjected it to every test known to me. Throughout my life it had made the days joyous. Doubt had fled. I possessed the Truth and understood, measurably, the pure and simple gospel of Jesus Christ.

"I had studied the gospel as carefully as any science. The literature of the Church I had acquired and read. During my spare time, day by day, I had increased my gospel learning. And I had put the gospel truth to work in daily life, and had never found it wanting.

"The claims of Joseph Smith the Prophet had been examined and weighed. No scientific claim had received a more thorough analysis. Everywhere the divine mission of the latter-day prophet was confirmed.

"The restored Church had been compared with other churches. Doctrine for doctrine, principle for principle, organization for organization, the churches had been placed side by side. Compared with the churches of the world, the Church of Jesus Christ, as restored through Joseph Smith, stood like a field of ripening grain by the side of scattering stalks.

"The stream of Church history since Jesus' day was muddy. The churches could not confirm the descent of their authority. The facts in recorded history proved the reality of the apostasy from the primitive faith, as taught by Jesus, the Christ. The restored Church alone possessed the priesthood of Almighty God" (pp. 158-59).

148

No one knows anything about his homeland simply because he was born a citizen thereof. He must learn. No one knows anything about Christ's work simply by being born a member of the Church, and often he knows little about it after years of unmotivated exposure in meetings or classes. He must learn. And learning involves self-investment and effort. The gospel should be studied "as carefully as any science." The "literature of the Church" must be "acquired and read." Our learning should be increased in our spare time "day by day." Then as we put the gospel truth to work in daily life, we will never find it wanting. We will be literate in the most important field of knowledge in the universe, knowledge for lack of which men and nations perish, in the light of which men and nations may be saved.

The Messenger in Preparation

The *message,* the *messenger*, and the *mission* . . . words with unique meaning in your life. Your generation is carrying the message—the word of the Lord. Among you are the special messengers of today and the real role players of tomorrow. Yours isn't just a time of preparing for the future of service. You are the generation with a mission to perform now. You may be ready for a formal call to a particular field of labor, or serving in youth missionary activities at home—either way you are in the picture. As a student, a summer worker, a helper at camp or a tender of tots, there are those to touch that only you can reach. To bring truth and awareness, light and understanding and a new knowledge of God and his Son to those who haven't known them is the message and the mission of your generation.

149

Health

Missionary work is extremely demanding and imposes heavy physical and emotional strains. One who is preparing for a mission call should be thinking of this.

A missionary who is not well cannot do the work, and his companion and others and the work itself all suffer serious interference. In many cases we can do something about improving our health.

Ask yourself these questions:

Do you have any serious problems with your health?

Can you work steadily and energetically over a prolonged period?

Do you understand and practice sound basic principles of nutrition, hygiene, sleep, and exercise?

Have you been involved with drugs in any illegal or inappropriate way?

Is your weight about what it should be?

Have you ever had a severe nervous or emotional disturbance or disorder?

Do you like people and enjoy being with them?

Are you sincerely, genuinely interested in others?

Can you accept them as they are, love them, and want to share your blessings with them?

In accepting ourselves and in accepting, appreciating, and serving our Father's other children, we are showing our love for him. This is one of the most important ways to be preparing to serve the Lord. Make and follow good health habits, and learn, by practice, to love and serve your fellowmen.

You are God's child. Like the sun and moon and stars—but in the most special sense—you are God's "creation." You have a right and a reason to be here. And unlike the sun, moon, and stars, you are an agent; you can think and decide and act.

Worthiness

Personal cleanliness and a clear conscience are indispensable for missionary happiness and effectiveness. You must make no mistake about that. And there can be no clear conscience for any of us without sincere repentance and conduct which is consistent with our high callings and holy professions.

Do you understand what it means to be morally clean?

Are you morally clean?

Have you ever been guilty of conduct which you understand to be immoral or improper or questionable? If so, have you followed the program of the Lord in making things right?

Do you understand the principle of repentance?

Have you been honest and honorable in your relationships with others?

Do you respect, honor, and obey the law?

Are you thoroughly converted to the Word of Wisdom?

Are you living it conscientiously, happily?

Are you dependable? Is your word important to you?

Do you keep your promise?

Will you follow counsel, accept instruction, obey established rules?

All these questions will help you assess your worthiness. If you are not worthy, now is the time to get yourself ready!

Education

The Lord has not chosen to call his servants exclusively from among the highly educated and specially trained. Whereas men might be inclined to concern themselves with the "countenance" (or perhaps the academic credentials) of a man, the story of the choosing of David teaches us that the Lord "looketh on the heart." (1 Samuel 16:7.)

When Christ selected those who were to walk and work with him in establishing his program on the earth, he went among simple, unsophisticated men. But those whom he chose were not weaklings; they were men of strong minds and strong characters, whose hearts could be educated to his way and the way and will of his Father.

Repeatedly in the era of restoration, the Lord has encouraged his followers to educate their minds and hearts. He has established broad fields of legitimate inquiry. (D&C 88:77-79; 90:15; 93:53.) And he has done this, he says, "That ye may be prepared in all things when I shall send you again to magnify the calling where-unto I have called you, and the mission with which I have commissioned you." (D&C 88:80.)

How is your educational preparation?

How much formal schooling have you had?

Did you do well in your studies? Do you love to learn?

Can you read well? Can you memorize efficiently?

Do you read? Are you regularly storing your mind with scriptures, wholesome thoughts, worthwhile poems?

Have you had any training or experience in a foreign language?

While the Lord does not choose his servants because of their formal academic training or degrees, a missionary who is alert and informed and educated and whose heart and mind and spirit are attuned to the Lord and his will is in an excellent position to succeed in his sacred commission.

152 Spirituality

God's truth can be known only through the Spirit of the Lord. This is the only way anyone can understand the gospel. Theologians who deal with the learned language and complex ideas of their profession but who do not have the Spirit cannot possibly know truth which can only come through that Spirit.

The humblest servant of God can know the truth through the Spirit.

With all other preparations, therefore, the most important readiness for any agent of the Master is to be in tune with the Spirit.

You have learned to "say your prayers." Do you pray often, "with real intent," talking with the Lord thoughtfully and humbly and gratefully?

Do you find your "closet" or "secret place" and talk out loud with the Lord? Have you told him what you want to be and want to do?

Do you acknowledge your faults and troubles to him and then seek to increase your faith and overcome your weaknesses?

Do you attend your meetings regularly? Do you practice controlling your mind while there, being prayerful, meditating?

When you partake of the sacrament of the Lord's Supper, are you worshiping?

Do you take part whenever asked and volunteer when someone is needed?

Are you negative and critical about others, especially those who have accepted heavy responsibilities and are trying to fulfil them?

Do you support your bishop and all others who lead?

Do you really love your Heavenly Father and his Son?

Do you truly try to serve him and keep his commandments?

Financial Competence

Along with all other costs, the cost of doing missionary work has risen sharply in recent years. Much more money is required to sustain a missionary than was previously needed. This very important consideration, therefore, needs the careful attention and preparation of every person who contemplates filling a mission.

Parents and families and prospective missionaries should be thinking and planning and saving well in advance.

Do you and your parents know how much a mission will cost?

Are you sensitive and mature enough to use frugally the sacred funds committed to missionary work by others?

Are you earning and saving at least part of the money needed to sustain you on a mission?

Are your parents able and planning to help you?

Will there be other sources of income to which you may look for help?

Do you appreciate the value of money?

Can you budget? Do without? Make do? Do over?

The Church expects that every missionary family will supply at least part of the support for its missionary. This is vitally important for the family and for the missionary and for the work.

Missionary work is a labor of love and unselfishness and derives no small part of its efficacy from the sacrifice and devotion of the people. It would be well if every missionary were able to support himself at least in part by funds he had earned himself and had saved for that special purpose.

If you are not ready financially, now is the time to prepare!

Desire

One who honorably fulfils a calling as a missionary must want to do the work and succeed in it. So, examine yourself—do you really want to go on a mission?

Do you have a testimony that this is the Lord's work, that it is vital for all men, and that it is your personal responsibility to see that others have a chance to hear the message?

Do you know how to work, to endure discouragements and disappointments and adverse circumstances courageously and maturely?

Are you ready and willing to "seek first the kingdom of God"? to be set apart for a time from the normal pursuits and ambitions and associations of your life? to give your whole heart, mind, strength, and loyalty to the sacred cause?

Will you commit yourself for the rest of your life to the high standards of responsibility and devotion expected of one who has been a missionary?

If the answers are affirmative, your foundation is firm; if they are not; it is time for you to prepare!

Preparation

One cannot teach that which one does not know. The messengers of the Lord go into the world to teach and testify and share the light of the gospel. They must know what they are talking about. Have you earnestly studied the gospel and prayed for a personal witness of its truthfulness? Have you earnestly "searched," "knocked," "asked," "sought"? Have you made a serious personal effort to understand the principles of salvation?

How much have you read of the history of the Church?

Have you ever made a serious, sustained effort to study the life of Jesus Christ?

Have you read the standard works of the Church?

Did you or do you attend seminary? institute?

Have you been active in your quorums and auxiliary organizations?

Do you know how to study? Do you know how to listen?

Can you organize a sermon or a lesson?

Do you read regularly and listen perceptively?

Are you prepared to teach the gospel and testify intelligently of its principles? A missionary must be.

If you are not prepared, now is the time!

The
Future
Youth
Holds

"WATCH THESE MORMONS. A century ago they founded an empire among the relentless wastes of a despised and neglected land. Today they are pioneering in the frontier of the spirit in the midst of a world that has lost its way."

—Dr. Marcus Bach, School of Religion, State University of Iowa.

Does this description fit you? Are you a pioneer on the frontier of the spirit? Living in a world of fear and discontent, of uncertainty and lack of faith, what can you do to help yourself and others meet the problems of our day?

Ask yourself these questions, and then consider these suggestions in answer.

Is there anything, really, that I personally can do to help my country and the world? Is there some contribution that I can make?

What can I do? What ought I to do? Do I have a responsibility to do something?

What should our attitude be in the face of this great responsibility?

"For God hath not given us the spirit of fear; but of power, and of love, and of a sound mind." (2 Timothy 1:7.)

" . . . Be strong and of a good courage; be not afraid, neither be thou dismayed: for the Lord thy God is with thee whithersoever thou goest." (Joshua 1:9.)

So . . . how may I accomplish this, my great responsibility? How may I overcome fear and merit this great gift of God—courage, and the spirit of power, love, and a sound mind?

So, What Can I Do?

1. I can love God and have faith in him.

I can do my best to be strong, and banish fear, radiate calm, confidence, stand steadfast and courageous.

But—how do I go about learning to love God and to serve him?

"Then one of them, which was a lawyer, asked him a question, tempting him, and saying, "Master, which is the great commandment in the law?

"Jesus said unto him, Thou shalt love the Lord thy God with all thy heart, and with all thy soul, and with all thy mind.

"This is the first and great commandment.

"And the second is like unto it, Thou shalt love thy neighbour as thyself.

"On these two commandments hang all the law and the prophets."

And Mark adds to Matthew 22:35-40, this sentence: *"There is none other commandment greater than these."* (Mark 12:31.)

So we learn to love God by serving him; and we serve him by serving his children, our brothers. Only by demonstrating love for my brother can I show my love for God.

2. I can seek to understand repentance, the great principle of growth.

And I can begin to repent wherein I have made mistakes and wherein I do now err.

But of what must I repent? I have committed no great sin.

"Woe unto you, scribes and Pharisees, hypocrites! for ye pay tithe . . . and have omitted the weightier matters of the law, judgment, mercy, and faith: these ought ye to have done, and not to leave the other undone." (Matthew 23:23.)

Begin now to overcome my sins, then, and to strengthen myself where I need it.

Start by standing myself up and stepping down to take an honest look at myself.

"These six things doth the Lord hate: yea, seven are an abomination to him:

"A proud look, a lying tongue, and hands that shed innocent blood,

"An heart that deviseth wicked imaginations, feet that be swift in running to mischief,

"A false witness that speaketh lies, and he that soweth discord among brethren." (Proverbs 6:16-19.)

3. I can seek more earnestly to know the commandments of God and to live them.

I can find attunement with God by eradicating static and interference within myself. I can seek to purify my heart, that my prayers may reach him, that he will be with me wherever I go, that I may stand with confidence in his presence.

"Verily I say, men should be anxiously engaged in a good cause, and do many things of their own free will, and bring to pass much righteousness;

"For the power is in them, wherein they are agents unto themselves. And inasmuch as men do good they shall in nowise lose their reward." (D&C 58:27-28.)

"Believe in God; believe that he is, and that he created all things, both in heaven and in earth; believe that he has all wisdom, and all power, both in heaven and in earth; believe that man doth not comprehend all the things which the Lord can comprehend.

"And again, believe that ye must repent of your sins and forsake them, and humble yourselves before God; and ask in sincerity of heart that he would forgive you; and now, if you believe all these things see that ye do them." (Mosiah 4:9-10.)

If We Do These Things

If we do these things, we will be "strong and of good courage; be not afraid, neither be thou dismayed: for the Lord thy God is with thee whithersoever thou goest." (Joshua 1:9.)

"For God hath not given us the spirit of fear; but of power, and of love, and of a sound mind." (2 Timothy 1:7.)

And it may well be that what we individually can do, if we will do it, may be the means of preserving our great land and of bringing God's purposes to fruition on his earth.

"Yea; and I say unto you that if it were not for the prayers of the righteous, who are now in the land, that ye would even now be visited with utter destruction; yet it would not be by flood, as were the people in the days of Noah, but it would be by famine, and by pestilence, and the sword. But it is by the prayers of the righteous that ye are spared." (Alma 10:22, 23.)

159

Be Ready

160

Jesus told the lawyer that the first and great commandment is to "love the Lord thy God with all thy heart, and with all thy soul, and with all thy mind.

"And the second is like unto it," he said. "Thou shalt love thy neighbour as thyself." (Matthew 22:37, 39.) All other commandments depend upon this.

In a generation represented by youth who refuse to whine and whimper in the face of great difficulties, who can thank God for trouble in their time if it has to come, there is great and glorious promise. But I believe the summation of the best in them, or in any of us, is in that attitude which motivated one of their number to say, "God, I am ready for you, if you are ready for me."

Have you said that, in your own way, and really meant it?

Whom Do You Hear?

The problems of our day are very great. Many of the voices we have traditionally been able to count on are silent or confused. In the world of theology and religion there is uncertainty and controversy. Faith seems to wane, spirits to sag. We worry about what men say. Perhaps it is time to cease to worry so much about what men say and ask ourselves. "What has God said?" More important than what our neighbors are doing, or what the rest are doing, is what God has done.

To God's Servants

Long ago there was a young man who, though "little in [his] own sight," was chosen king of all Israel. The humble Saul was ready for God; and when the prophet of God had anointed him, he "turned into another man." The Spirit of the Lord came upon him. "God gave him another heart." While he listened to the Lord and his prophets he led with great strength. When he became willful and stubborn and rebellious he ceased to be useful and he lost his place. "For rebellion is as the sin of witchcraft, and stubbornness is as iniquity and idolatry." (See 1 Samuel 10, 15.)

A young man named Solomon loved the Lord and earnestly said to him, "I am but a little child: I know not how to go out or come in." (1 Kings 3:7.) He asked God for an understanding heart that he might discern between good and bad, and he was so blessed. Only when he ceased to listen to the Lord and became a law unto himself did he lose his gift and his place.

On the other hand, young Samuel learned and remembered all his life to say, "Speak, Lord; for thy servant heareth," and became a great power for good and a chosen instrument in the hands of the Lord. (1 Samuel 3:9.)

Young Joseph, sold into Egypt as a slave, remembered who he was and what he had been taught, even in the terrible temptations of Potiphar's household, and lived to serve and save his people.

A humble young Joshua presented himself to the Lord pleading for help, and the Lord said to him, "As I was with Moses, so I will be with thee: I will not fail thee, nor forsake thee. . .

"Be strong and of a good courage; be not afraid, neither be thou dismayed: for the Lord thy God is with thee whithersoever thou goest." (Joshua 1:5, 9.)

God has spoken and still speaks, and the message is clear.

"Send Me"

Beyond these, and above them all, is the scriptural account of a choice Son of God, knowing the need for a messenger from God to man on a mission requiring great faith and courage and sacrifice, saying to his Heavenly Father: "Send me."

He delivered his message, completed his mission, gave his life. In his moment of great agony and torment before Calvary, he laid his life on the altar and said, as we have learned:

"O my Father, if it be possible, let this cup pass from me: nevertheless not as I will, but as thou wilt." (Matthew 26:39.)

Was this the spirit exercised by one of his humble young disciples in a grove of trees in Colorado a little time ago as he prayed, "God, I am ready for you, if you are ready for me"?

To You, Personally

162

To the younger generation, our admonition and loving invitation is that you accept the responsibilities of your great promise. Continue to prepare for the duties of the day and the morrow. Get the help of the Lord. Appreciate your heritage. See the great goodness around you. Forgive us our trespasses and improve upon our performance. Respect our earnest efforts to protect and perpetuate the good things of life for you. Have a decent respect for generations yet unborn. Know that *your* decisions will materially affect the opportunities open to *them*. Build more strongly than we have the foundations for a decent future for all mankind. Keep the idealisms of the fathers of your freedom and the fathers of your faith. Accept the implications of your freedom; make the difficult choices when they are right, and act on them, even if you must stand alone.

Be Ready

Through search and service and reverence, through a life of personal cleanliness and consideration and caring, through faith and trust in God, you can be ready for him. Tell him you are, and he will surely give you the strength and courage and quality to live with contribution and meaning and with great personal satisfaction in this, his world.

Index

163

164

165

166